Automated Diagnostic Systems for Diabetic Retinopathy

Bush William

TABLE OF CONTENTS

Chapter 1
Introduction

CHAPTER 1
INTRODUCTION

1.1 Introduction

Diabetic Retinopathy (DR) is a major cause of vision loss and blindness in working-age adults globally. It is a microvascular complication of diabetes mellitus that affects the retinal blood vessels, leading to progressive damage if left undetected or untreated [1]. Early detection of DR is crucial as timely intervention can significantly slow disease progression, prevent vision loss, and improve patients' quality of life. With the increasing global prevalence of diabetes, there is a growing demand for efficient screening strategies that can accurately identify early signs of DR before irreversible retinal damage occurs. Additionally, predicting the progression of DR can guide personalized treatment strategies, helping clinicians prioritize high-risk patients and optimize care management.

Various modalities are employed for the detection of DR, ranging from traditional clinical examination techniques such as fundus photography and optical coherence tomography (OCT) to more advanced imaging modalities like fluorescein angiography [2]. Each modality provides unique information about retinal changes, enabling comprehensive assessment of disease severity. Alongside imaging, a variety of detection methods have been developed, including manual grading by ophthalmologists, automated image processing techniques, and machine learning-based approaches. These methods aim to improve diagnostic accuracy, reduce screening time, and facilitate large-scale population screening. Understanding the strengths and limitations of different modalities and detection techniques is critical for developing effective DR monitoring systems and enhancing early diagnosis and progression prediction.

1.2 Overview of Diabetic Retinopathy

DR begins as a disease of the retinal capillaries and may eventually affect larger veins and arteries. The earliest changes involve the loss of pericytes, which support vessel walls, causing the walls to weaken and leak plasma into surrounding tissue. This weakening often results in microaneurysms, small bulges along the capillaries. Plasma leakage can lead to widespread retinal swelling, while exudates solid fat deposits from dying phagocytic cells form at the edges of these swollen areas, often appearing in ring-like patterns around clusters of microaneurysms. Such lesions are classified as background retinopathy and usually do not require treatment unless they encroach upon the fovea. Alongside leakage, blood vessel blockage may occur due to thickened basement membranes, sticky red blood cells, and increased platelet aggregation. These blockages reduce oxygen supply to parts of the retina, prompting the formation of new capillaries, known as intra-retinal microvascular abnormalities, while small hemorrhages appear and larger vessels, especially veins, begin to dilate and deform, signaling pre-proliferative retinopathy.

In advanced stages, extensive areas of avascular retina trigger the release of growth factors that stimulate neovascularization to supply oxygen to hypoxic regions. Unfortunately, these new vessels grow chaotically, often leading to retinal detachment, traction, and sudden vision loss hallmarks of proliferative retinopathy. Because this phase progresses rapidly and can have catastrophic consequences, early detection is critical. Regular screening is therefore essential, but manual evaluation is costly and labor-intensive. To overcome these challenges, automated detection systems have been developed that analyze retinal images to identify DR-related changes. These computerized methods enable earlier diagnosis, reduce screening costs, and form the basis of the automated DR detection approach presented in this study.

1.2.1 Anatomy of Eye

The eye, a highly specialized photoreceptive organ, forms a central part of the visual system along with its accessory structures and the optic nerves that transmit information to the brain. It converts environmental light into signals detected by rod and cone cells in the retina, which are then interpreted by the brain as vision. Structurally, the eyeball is nearly spherical, about 20 mm in diameter, and composed of three main layers or tunics: the fibrous tunic (sclera and cornea), the vascular tunic (choroid, ciliary body, and iris), and the nervous tunic (retina). The sclera, the firm white outer layer, protects the eye, maintains its shape, and serves as a muscle attachment point, while the transparent cornea at the front allows light to enter and performs initial focusing. The vascular tunic houses most of the eye's blood vessels, with the choroid supplying 90% of its blood, while the ciliary body supports the lens for precise focusing and the iris controls pupil size to regulate light reaching the retina. Filling the central cavity, the vitreous humor, a clear jelly-like fluid, maintains intraocular pressure, holds the lens and retina in place, and contributes to the eye's refractive power. Abnormal increases in intraocular pressure, known as glaucoma, can threaten vision and require urgent medical care. The anatomy of the eye is illustrated in **Figure 1.1.**

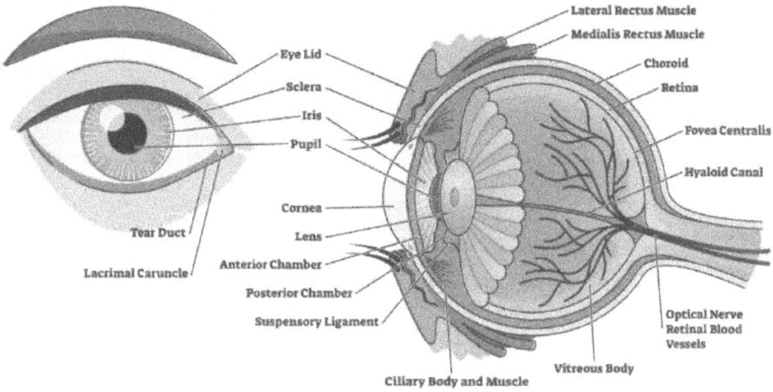

Figure 1.1: Representation of Anatomy of Eye

1.2.1.1 Eye Ball

The human eyeball has an approximate diameter of 2.5 cm and a volume of 6.5 ml, comprising two main spherical components: the smaller, highly curved cornea at the front and the larger sclera forming the posterior portion. The eye is built from three primary tissue layers and contains the anterior and posterior chambers, the lens, and the aqueous and vitreous humors. The outer layer includes the opaque sclera, which provides structural support and protection, and the transparent cornea that permits light entry. The cornea, covering about one-sixth of the eyeball's circumference with a radius of 7.8 mm, is avascular and consists of an outer connective tissue matrix and an inner single cell layer. The anterior chamber, located between the cornea and lens, is filled with aqueous humor, a watery fluid that maintains intraocular pressure and nourishes the cornea and lens. The iris, a thin, contractile, colored disk, regulates light entry through the pupil, which dilates in dim light and contracts under bright conditions.

The lens is a transparent biconvex structure behind the iris and in front of the vitreous body, is composed of organized lens fibers and serves as the primary focusing component of the optical system. Posterior to the lens lies the vitreous chamber, the largest cavity of the eye, filled with gel-like vitreous humor that holds the retina against the choroid for a clear visual plane and contains phagocytes to remove debris. The retina, the innermost layer, occupies the posterior three-quarters of the eyeball and converts visual images into neural impulses for transmission to the brain. Lining the internal scleral surface, the choroid is highly vascularized, supplying nutrients to the retina and containing melanocytes to absorb stray light and prevent internal scattering. The sclera, dense with collagen fibers and fibroblasts, surrounds most of the eyeball, anchoring the eye muscles and maintaining shape and rigidity to protect internal structures.

1.2.1.2 Retina

The retina is a specialized, multilayered structure situated between the choroid and the vitreous body, covering about two-thirds of the inner surface of the eyeball [71]. It is highly sensitive to light and responsible for converting visual stimuli into neural signals [85]. The central region, called the macula, contains the fovea at its center a small depression critical for sharp, detailed vision [81]. Near the optic disc, a pale, slightly raised area about 1.8 mm in diameter, all blood vessels enter and retinal nerve fibers exit, forming the optic nerve; this region lacks photoreceptors and is therefore known as the blind spot. The retina varies in thickness from roughly 100 μm at the periphery to 230 μm near the optic nerve head, and its surface is topographically uneven, reflecting the foveal depression and optic disc elevation.

Structurally, the retina is composed of several layers that together detect and transmit visual information. The innermost Internal Limiting Membrane (ILM) is a smooth basement layer formed by Müller cells, beneath which lies the Nerve Fiber

Layer (NFL) containing ganglion cell axons that allow light to pass through. The neural retina houses photoreceptors rods for low-light and motion detection, and cones for color and fine spatial resolution. These photoreceptors connect to bipolar and horizontal cells in the outer plexiform layer, enabling signal integration and transmission toward the inner layers of the retina.

The Retinal Pigment Epithelium (RPE) forms the deepest layer, consisting of pigmented hexagonal cells that absorb scattered light, protect against photo-damage, and maintain the blood-retina barrier. The RPE, separated from the choroid by Bruch's membrane, also facilitates nutrient and water transport between the neural retina and choroid, keeping the retina attached and nourished. Together, these layers form a vertically organized network, transmitting visual signals from rods and cones to bipolar cells, then to ganglion cells, and finally through the nerve fiber layer to the brain for image processing.

1.2.1.3 Choroid

The choroid is a blood vessel-rich layer situated between the sclera and retina, lying beneath the retinal pigment epithelium (RPE) and separated by Bruch's membrane. Its primary function is to supply oxygen and nutrients to the inner layers of the sensory retina, particularly those closest to it. The choroid is thickest at the posterior pole, around 250 μm, and thins to approximately 100 μm near the ciliary body, reflecting the varying metabolic demands of different retinal regions. It contains a dense network of fenestrated capillaries called the choriocapillaris, along with progressively larger veins arranged in layers.

The choroid is structurally made up of three primary layers. The outermost layer is supra-choroid (lamina fusca), houses nerves as well as the long and short posterior ciliary arteries, which supply blood to the choriocapillaris. The middle layer houses blood vessels, divided into large veins leading to the vortex veins, medium-sized veins and arterioles, and the innermost layer of fenestrated capillaries forming the choriocapillaris. Bruch's membrane lies at the innermost boundary, anchoring the RPE and maintaining close contact between the retina and choroid.

The choroid works in coordination with the retinal and uveal circulations to maintain retinal homeostasis. Branches of the ophthalmic artery, including the short and long ciliary arteries, feed the uveal tract, while the venous drainage occurs through vortex veins that perforate the sclera. Continuous perfusion from both the uveal and retinal circulations is essential for normal retinal function, although the fovea relies primarily on choroidal flow due to its lack of retinal vessels. Overall, the choroid provides approximately 90% of the eye's total blood supply, supporting photoreceptor metabolism and visual function.

1.2.1.4 Retinal Pigment Epithelium

The retinal pigment epithelium (RPE) primarily transports fluids and nutrients to the rods and cones of the sensory retina [81]. It is rich in melanin, which minimizes reflection and scattering of incoming light, preventing it from bouncing back onto the retina. While this slightly reduces the total light reaching photoreceptors, it enhances image clarity and sharpness by limiting light scattering.

1.2.1.5 Retinal Circulation

The retina is supplied with blood by two primary sources: the choroid through the retinal pigment epithelium and the central retinal artery, which enters at the optic disc and branches into four parts, dividing the retina into quadrants. Retinal arteries and veins lie on the surface within the nerve fiber layer, while capillaries descend to supply the outer half of the sensory retina, stopping at the middle limiting membrane. Since there are no connections between retinal blood vessels, any blockage in the main artery or its branches can cause ischemia, leading to severe retinal damage.

1.2.1.6 Anatomical regions of the retina

Anatomically, the retina can be divided into key regions across its inner surface such as macula, fovea, and optic disc.

- The macula is the central area responsible for sharp, detailed vision, roughly 1.5 mm in diameter, and contains the foveal avascular zone of about 0.5 mm.
- At the center of this zone lies the fovea, a 0.4 mm region where the retina thins to approximately 75 μm and contains only cone cells, providing high

visual acuity and color perception in bright light. In low-light conditions, peripheral rod cells take over to enhance night vision.

- The optic disc, located about 6 mm nasal to the fovea, is where the retinal nerve fibers converge to form the optic nerve and contains no photoreceptors, creating the blind spot.

1.3 Importance of Early detection and Progression Prediction of diabetic retinopathy

Diabetic Retinopathy (DR) growths through different stages, starting with Non-Proliferative Diabetic Retinopathy (NPDR), where the retinal blood vessels become damaged, leading to microaneurysms, leakage, and swelling, potentially causing macular edema. In this early stage, vision may not be significantly affected. As the condition advances, it progresses to Proliferative Diabetic Retinopathy (PDR), where new, fragile blood vessels grow in the retina, increasing the risk of vitreous hemorrhage, retinal detachment, and severe vision loss. The severity of DR is classified into mild, moderate, severe NPDR, and PDR, with diabetic macular edema (DME) being a major cause of vision impairment [73]. Early detection and treatment are crucial in managing DR and preventing irreversible vision loss.

1.3.1 Stages of DR

Diabetic Retinopathy progresses through two primary stages such as i) Non-Proliferative Diabetic Retinopathy (NPDR) and ii) Proliferative Diabetic Retinopathy (PDR) [74]. When retinal blood vessels are damaged and leak fluid, NPDR develops, causing retinal swelling. This stage may show hemorrhages, exudates, inflammation, and minor vascular changes. In some cases, abnormal vessels form, leading to PDR, a severe stage that can cause significant vision loss. Since diabetic retinopathy is progressive, early detection and regular monitoring are essential to protect vision.

1.3.1.1 Non-Proliferative Diabetic Retinopathy (NPDR)

NPDR is the early stage of diabetic retinopathy, where retinal blood vessels swell and may form microaneurysms [80]. These vessels can leak fluid, causing swelling in the retina, particularly in the macula, leading to macular edema. Vision may become blurred, often described as looking through water. Blocked vessels, known as muscular ischemia, reduce blood flow to the retina. Tiny deposits called exudates may form, and fatty deposits can persist, further impairing vision. As the condition progresses, blood vessels may start bleeding within the retina. Early detection and monitoring are essential to prevent vision loss.

1.3.1.1.1 Types of NPDR

NPDR is classified into three stages: a) Mild NPDR, b) Moderate NPDR, and c) Severe NPDR.

a) **Mild NPDR:** Microaneurysms begin to form in the retinal blood vessels at this stage, sometimes causing fluid to leak into the retina. These appear as small, balloon-like expansions.

b) **Moderate NPDR:** With disease progression, the retinal blood vessels may become enlarged and lose their ability to deliver sufficient blood. If left untreated, moderate NPDR can progress into diabetic macular edema, which severely impacts vision. Around 50% of DR patients develop macular edema. Mild and moderate NPDR are typically referred to as "early DR."

c) **Severe NPDR:** In severe NPDR, the retinal blood supply is substantially disrupted, causing extensive damage to the blood vessels.

1.3.2 Proliferative Diabetic Retinopathy (PDR)

PDR is the advanced stage of diabetic retinopathy, where fragile new blood vessels (neovascularization) form on the retina [80]. These vessels can bleed into the vitreous, causing floaters and, in severe cases, vision loss or blindness [84]. Scar tissue may develop, pulling on the retina and risking retinal detachment. PDR requires prompt treatment to prevent permanent vision damage.

Therefore, the progression of these stages in diabetic retinopathy highlights the critical need for early detection and prediction of disease progression.

Early detection of DR is crucial because retinal damage is often irreversible once the disease reaches advanced stages. Mild DR may be asymptomatic, but if left untreated, it can progress to proliferative diabetic retinopathy (PDR), causing neovascularization and vitreous hemorrhage, or diabetic macular edema (DME) [88], leading to central vision loss. Detecting DR early enables timely interventions like laser photocoagulation, intravitreal injections, or vitrectomy, preventing severe vision loss. Early detection is also cost-effective, reducing the need for expensive treatments for advanced DR, and improves patient outcomes by promoting better systemic control of blood sugar, blood pressure, and cholesterol. Screening programs, including AI-assisted retinal imaging, are particularly valuable for mass detection in resource-limited or remote areas. Predicting DR progression allows clinicians to estimate how quickly the disease may worsen, enabling proactive and personalized management. Patients at high risk of rapid progression can receive early treatment, while low-risk patients may be monitored less intensively, optimizing healthcare resources. Risk stratification identifies slow and rapid progressors, guiding lifestyle interventions, tighter glycemic control, and targeted medical care. Progression prediction also plays a key role in clinical research, where AI models can analyze large datasets to uncover patterns, evaluate therapies, and identify new risk factors to slow DR progression.

1.4 Different Modalities used for Detection

Detection of diabetic retinopathy relies on imaging the retina to identify structural changes, lesions, and vascular abnormalities caused by prolonged hyperglycemia. Several imaging modalities are used in clinical practice and research, ranging from conventional fundus photography to advanced techniques like Optical Coherence Tomography (OCT) and fluorescein angiography [82]. These modalities vary in invasiveness, resolution, cost, and suitability for automated analysis.

1.4.1 Fundus Photography

Fundus photography is used for DR detection. It involves capturing a high-resolution image of the retina using a fundus camera. This non-invasive method provides a clear, color-accurate view of the retina, including critical areas such as the macula, optic disc, and blood vessels.

Key Uses in DR Detection:

- Lesion Detection: It helps in detecting characteristic DR lesions like microaneurysms, hemorrhages, exudates, and cotton-wool spots.
- Screening and Grading: It is primarily used for screening purposes in large populations and for grading DR based on the severity (mild, moderate, severe NPDR, or PDR).
- Longitudinal Monitoring: Fundus images are stored over time, allowing for the monitoring of DR progression or remission.

Advantages:

- Non-invasive and relatively simple to perform.
- Wide availability and lower cost compared to other techniques.
- Permanent record of retinal images that can be compared over time.
- Compatibility with AI-based automation for faster DR detection and classification.

Limitations:

- Limited depth information: Fundus photography provides only a 2D image, which lacks depth resolution.
- Peripheral Lesions: Standard fundus photography has a narrow field of view, which might miss peripheral lesions, especially in advanced stages of DR.
- Subjectivity in Grading: Manual interpretation and grading of DR severity can vary across different practitioners, leading to potential misclassification.

1.4.2 Optical Coherence Tomography (OCT)

OCT is an advanced imaging modality that uses light waves to produce high-resolution cross-sectional images of the retina [83]. It allows visualization of individual retinal layers and is particularly effective in detecting changes in retinal thickness.

Key Uses in DR Detection:

- Macular Edema Detection: OCT is invaluable for identifying macular edema, the swelling of the retina due to fluid leakage, which is a common complication of DR.

- Retinal Layer Analysis: It helps in detecting structural damage in the retina caused by DR, such as thickening of the retinal nerve fiber layer or changes in the inner retinal layers.
- Monitoring Treatment Response: OCT is used to evaluate the effectiveness of treatments like anti-VEGF therapy and laser photocoagulation.

Advantages:

- High resolution and ability to visualize individual retinal layers.
- Non-invasive with minimal discomfort for the patient.
- Provides detailed quantitative data such as retinal thickness and volume.
- Ideal for detecting subtle retinal changes that may not be visible on fundus photographs.

Limitations:

- Costly equipment and relatively expensive for routine use.
- Limited field of view: OCT provides a small area of the retina, meaning peripheral lesions may be missed.
- The need for trained personnel to interpret results accurately.

1.4.3 Fluorescein Angiography (FA)

Fluorescein angiography involves the intravenous injection of fluorescein dye, followed by photography of the retina using a special camera [84] [89]. The dye illuminates the retinal blood vessels, allowing visualization of blood flow and leakage.

Key Uses in DR Detection:

- Microaneurysm Detection: FA is extremely sensitive in identifying microaneurysms, which are a hallmark of DR, even before they become visible on fundus images.
- Leakage Assessment: It helps in detecting vascular leakage and impaired blood flow, both of which are critical in DR progression.
- Neovascularization: FA is essential for detecting neovascularization (the growth of new, abnormal blood vessels) in proliferative DR (PDR), which can cause bleeding and retinal detachment.

Advantages:

- Gold standard for detecting vascular changes and abnormalities in DR.
- Allows visualization of blood vessel leakage and the perfusion status of retinal tissues.
- Provides a dynamic view of the retina and retinal circulation, including changes in real-time.

Limitations:

- Invasive procedure involving the injection of dye, which carries a risk of allergic reactions or complications.
- Requires specialized equipment and trained personnel to interpret the results.
- Time-consuming and not ideal for frequent monitoring of DR.

1.4.4 Fundus Autofluorescence (FAF)

Fundus autofluorescence is a non-invasive imaging technique that captures the natural fluorescence emitted by retinal pigments, mainly lipofuscin [75]. This allows visualization of stressed or damaged retinal tissue without the need for any contrast agents.

Key Uses in DR Detection:

- Early Retinal Stress Detection: FAF is highly effective in identifying areas of retinal dysfunction or early damage that may not be visible on fundus photographs.
- Macular Disease Monitoring: It is particularly useful in detecting early changes in the macula, which are crucial for DR and macular diseases.
- Lesion Detection: FAF highlights areas of exudates or ischemia, making it a useful tool for identifying both early and late-stage DR.

Advantages:

- Non-invasive and quick with no need for dye injections.
- Sensitive to retinal stress and early-stage changes that are hard to detect with other modalities.
- Can detect both hyperfluorescence (e.g., exudates) and hypofluorescence (e.g., ischemia or atrophy).

Limitations:

- Limited vascular information compared to FA or OCT.
- The technique is sensitive to noise, and interpreting low contrast images can be challenging.
- Limited use in peripheral regions of the retina.

1.4.5 Optical Coherence Tomography Angiography (OCTA)

OCTA is a non-invasive imaging technique that uses motion contrast to visualize retinal and choroidal blood flow [82] [87]. It creates high-resolution 3D images of retinal vasculature without the need for contrast dye.

Key Uses in DR Detection:

- Microvasculature Imaging: OCTA can visualize retinal capillaries, providing insights into the early stages of DR and identifying capillary dropout, a hallmark of DR.
- Detecting Neovascularization: It helps in identifying neovascularization in PDR, where fragile new blood vessels can cause vision-threatening complications.
- Monitoring Treatment: OCTA is also used to monitor neovascular activity and the effectiveness of treatments like anti-VEGF.

Advantages:

- Non-invasive and fast, with no dye required.
- Provides 3D visualization of retinal and choroidal blood vessels.
- Can detect neovascularization and microvascular changes early on.
- No risk of allergic reactions or dye-related complications.

Limitations:

- Limited field of view compared to wide-field FA.
- Susceptible to motion artifacts, especially when the patient is unable to maintain a stable gaze.
- Relatively expensive compared to other imaging techniques.

1.4.6 Fundus Fluorescence Lifetime Imaging (FLIM)

FLIM is an emerging technique that measures the fluorescence decay of retinal pigments, primarily focusing on lipofuscin and NADH. The decay time can be indicative of metabolic changes and tissue health.

Key Uses in DR Detection:

- Early Detection of Retinal Damage: FLIM can detect subtle metabolic changes in the retina before physical lesions or structural changes are visible.
- Assessing Retinal Metabolism: It helps monitor changes in retinal oxidative stress and tissue hypoxia, which can be an early sign of DR.

Advantages:

- Non-invasive and sensitive to early biochemical changes.
- Can detect early metabolic or functional changes in the retina, which can lead to earlier detection of DR.
- Label-free imaging, meaning no contrast agents are needed.

Limitations:

- Not widely available and mostly used in research settings.
- Requires specialized equipment and expertise for interpretation.
- High complexity and expensive.

1.4.7 Multimodal Imaging

Multimodal imaging combines multiple imaging modalities to leverage their strengths and overcome their individual limitations. This approach provides a more comprehensive view of the retina, improving diagnostic accuracy.

Key Uses in DR Detection:

- Comprehensive Assessment: By combining modalities like OCT, FA, and fundus photography, multimodal imaging can assess both vascular and structural changes, offering a holistic view of DR.
- Improved Diagnosis and Monitoring: Multimodal approaches allow clinicians to monitor disease progression more accurately and predict future complications like macular edema or neovascularization.

Advantages:

- Enhanced diagnostic accuracy through complementary information from different imaging modalities.
- Provides comprehensive monitoring of DR stages, allowing for personalized treatment plans.
- Improved detection of early and subtle changes, which might be missed by a single imaging modality.

Limitations:

- Expensive and time-consuming due to the need for multiple devices and extended analysis time.
- Requires integration of data from different modalities, which can be challenging without proper software and expertise.
- May not be readily accessible in resource-limited settings.

Each imaging modality has its strengths and limitations, and the choice of modality often depends on the clinical scenario, available resources, and desired outcome. Combining these techniques, especially through multimodal imaging, offers the most comprehensive approach to diagnosing, monitoring, and treating diabetic retinopathy.

1.5 Different Methods used for Detection

The detection of Diabetic Retinopathy (DR) involves various advanced methods that help in identifying the disease at early stages and classifying it for effective treatment. These methods range from traditional manual techniques to advanced machine learning (ML) and deep learning (DL) algorithms. Below are some key methods used for DR detection.

Automatic detection of diabetic retinopathy (DR) from digital fundus images has seen significant progress in recent years. Digital fundus images play a crucial role in DR classification, often utilizing various color spaces and segmented regions to enhance. The presence of DR is identified through characteristic lesions observed in fundus photographs. After detecting DR, different classifiers are employed to categorize the disease into its respective stages.

1.5.1 Classification Techniques

Image classification involves extracting information from a segmented image to determine whether a disease is present. The outcomes of classification are often evaluated via metrics like accuracy, specificity, and sensitivity. Practical experience in image classification typically includes:

- Training a classifier for two distinct image classes (e.g., —good‖ vs. —bad‖).
- Evaluating classifier performance using accuracy, sensitivity, and specificity.
- Experimenting with different visual representations for feature vectors.
- Obtaining and preparing training data for new classifiers.

In medical imaging, machine learning approaches are widely used for classification. These methods are broadly divided into:

i) Supervised Classification-where the training set contains labeled data.

ii) Unsupervised Classification-where the training set has no predefined labels.

Common classifiers include SVM, Relevance Vector Machine, Extreme Learning Machine, k-Nearest Neighbor, MLFFNN, Naive Bayes, Decision Tree, Ensemble Classifier, and Logistic Regression. Supervised methods dominate in DR classification, while unsupervised approaches include K-means clustering, mixture model clustering, hierarchical clustering, neural networks, and GANs. Classification techniques are applied to categorize fundus images into different stages of DR. Among the commonly used approaches are Multiclass SVM, Hybrid Kernel SVM, and Bag of Visual Words-based SVM.

1.5.1.1 Machine Learning-Based Models for DR Detection

Machine Learning (ML) has significantly advanced the detection and diagnosis of Diabetic Retinopathy (DR) [79]. ML-based models leverage algorithms to automatically analyze retinal images and identify signs of DR, providing faster, accurate, and scalable solutions for screening and diagnosis. These models can classify retinal images into various DR stages, from no DR to proliferative stages, and are especially useful in large-scale screening programs.

1.5.1.1.1 Overview of ML for DR Detection

Machine learning algorithms learn from historical data, allowing them to identify patterns and make predictions about unseen data. In the case of DR, ML models are typically trained using a large dataset of labeled retinal images (images that are already categorized according to DR severity). Once trained, these models can automatically assess new images, classifying them into different stages of DR or even detecting early signs that might be missed by human examiners.

The most commonly used ML techniques for DR detection are supervised learning models, where the algorithm learns from labeled data, and unsupervised learning models, where the algorithm tries to identify patterns in the data without predefined labels.

1.5.1.1.2 Common Machine Learning Techniques for DR Detection

Several ML techniques are used for DR detection, each with its strengths and weaknesses. Below are some of the most popular approaches:

1.5.1.1.2.1 SVM

SVM is a supervised learning algorithm used for both classification and regression. It is particularly useful for binary classification tasks, like distinguishing among healthy and DR-affected retinas. In SVM, retinal images are represented as points in an n-dimensional feature space, and the algorithm finds a hyperplane that maximally separates the two classes (DR and non-DR).

In SVM, each data point is represented in an n-dimensional feature space, and classification is achieved by identifying a hyperplane that separates the classes. The binary form of SVM outputs either a positive or negative class. SVM maximizes the margin between classes, supporting high generalization and efficient learning of non-linear functions. It is a non-probabilistic linear classifier, as the feature values fully determine the data point's placement in the feature space.

Advantages of SVM:

- High Dimensionality: Effective in spaces with many features, useful in tasks like document or image classification.

- Memory Efficiency: Only a subset of training points (support vectors) is used for decision-making.
- Versatility: Kernel functions allow modeling of non-linear decision boundaries, improving classification performance.

1.5.1.1.2.2 Hybrid Kernel-Based SVM

Hybrid kernel SVMs extend SVM for non-linear classification, useful when training data are not linearly separable. A kernel function acts as a hyper-surface that separates input data into two classes while minimizing the number of support vectors required. Common kernel types include Radial Basis Function (RBF), polynomial, spline, and multilayer perceptron, along with customized hybrid kernels derived from modifications of standard ones. Training is performed on a subset of images, with the remaining used for testing.

1.5.1.1.2.3 Bag of Visual Words-Based SVM

The Bag of Visual Words (BoVW) approach is widely used in computer vision for image classification. It can detect objects regardless of their position or orientation. The BoVW process involves:

- Identifying the image and extracting key features.
- Generating a codebook and constructing a histogram of code word occurrences.
- Representing each training image as a vector, classifying it against positive and negative examples, and applying the trained classifier to test images.

Advantages of Bag of Visual Words:

- Robust to changes in object position and orientation.
- Produces fixed-length vectors regardless of the number of features detected.
- Highly effective in classifying images according to their contents, often outperforming other classification methods.

1.5.1.2 Deep Learning-Based Detection of Diabetic Retinopathy

Deep Learning (DL) has emerged as a powerful approach for automatic detection and classification of diabetic retinopathy (DR) from fundus images [77].

Unlike traditional machine learning, DL methods automatically extract relevant features from images without the need for manual feature engineering. Convolutional Neural Networks (CNNs) are the most commonly used DL architecture for DR detection due to their ability to learn hierarchical image features efficiently [76].

1.5.1.2.1 Convolutional Neural Networks (CNNs)

CNNs are specialized neural networks designed for image analysis [86]. They consist of convolutional layers that extract spatial features, pooling layers that reduce dimensionality, and fully connected layers that perform classification [90]. In DR detection, CNNs can identify lesions such as microaneurysms, hemorrhages, and exudates, and classify fundus images into different stages: NPDR (mild, moderate, severe) and PDR.

Advantages of CNNs:

- Automatic Feature Extraction: No need for manual segmentation or feature engineering.
- High Accuracy: Capable of learning complex patterns and subtle variations in retinal images.
- Scalability: Can handle large datasets effectively, improving performance as more data are added.

Popular DL Architectures for DR Detection [78]

- AlexNet and VGGNet: Early CNN models used for DR detection, effective for classification but require significant computational resources.
- ResNet [78] (Residual Networks): Introduces residual connections to prevent vanishing gradient problems, enabling very deep networks for higher accuracy.
- Inception Networks: Combines multiple filter sizes in a single layer to capture features at different scales, improving detection of small retinal lesions.
- DenseNet: Uses dense connections between layers to enhance feature reuse and gradient flow, improving performance on limited datasets.

Transfer Learning for DR Detection

Due to the limited availability of labeled retinal images, transfer learning is commonly applied. Pre-trained CNNs on large datasets (like ImageNet) are fine-tuned on DR fundus images. This approach reduces training time and improves classification accuracy.

DL-Based End-to-End DR Detection Pipeline

- Image Preprocessing: Resize, normalize, and enhance contrast of fundus images.
- Feature Extraction: CNN automatically extracts hierarchical features from the images.
- Classification: Fully connected layers or softmax layers classify images into DR stages.
- Evaluation: Performance is measured using metrics like accuracy, sensitivity, specificity, and AUC (Area Under the ROC Curve).

Advanced DL Techniques

1) Attention Mechanisms: Focus the network on critical retinal regions, such as lesions, improving detection accuracy.

2) Generative Adversarial Networks (GANs): Generate synthetic fundus images to augment limited datasets.

3) Hybrid Models: Combine CNNs with recurrent neural networks (RNNs) or transformers to capture spatial and contextual relationships in retinal images.

1.6 Research Motivation

The increasing prevalence of diabetes worldwide has led to a corresponding rise in diabetic retinopathy (DR), a major cause of vision impairment and blindness. Early detection of DR is critical because the disease often progresses silently in its initial stages, and timely intervention can prevent irreversible retinal damage. Despite advancements in ophthalmology, many patients remain undiagnosed until the disease reaches advanced stages, primarily due to limitations in accessibility to specialized eye care and the subtlety of early retinal changes. This research is motivated by the urgent need for accurate, timely, and scalable approaches for early detection and progression prediction of DR, which can improve patient outcomes and reduce the healthcare burden associated with diabetes-related vision loss.

Another motivating factor is the diverse array of imaging modalities and detection methods available, each with unique advantages and issues. Traditional methods like fundus photography and OCT, provide detailed structural information about the retina, while emerging modalities offer functional insights. Detection methods range from manual grading by ophthalmologists to automated image analysis and machine learning-based predictive models. However, challenges like variability in image quality, inter-observer discrepancies, and the complexity of disease progression prediction hinder widespread and efficient implementation. This thesis is driven by the need to systematically explore these modalities and detection methods, aiming to develop robust frameworks that can enhance early diagnosis, accurately predict disease progression, and ultimately support better clinical decision-making in diabetic retinopathy management.

1.7 Research Objectives

The key objectives addressed in this thesis include:

- To develop a novel framework for the early detection of diabetic retinopathy using advanced imaging and analysis techniques.
- To implement predictive models for assessing the progression of diabetic retinopathy and identifying high-risk patients.
- To explore and evaluate different imaging modalities, such as fundus photography, optical coherence tomography (OCT), and fluorescein angiography, for accurate DR detection.
- To investigate various detection methods, including manual grading, automated image processing, and machine learning-based approaches, to improve diagnostic accuracy and efficiency.
- To analyze and compare the performance of different modalities and methods in terms of sensitivity, specificity, and reliability for DR screening and progression prediction.

- To provide insights and recommendations for integrating early detection and progression prediction systems into clinical practice, enhancing patient care and preventive strategies.

1.8 Contributions of the thesis

This thesis makes the following key contributions:

- **Chapter 2** reviews the key concepts and challenges of diabetic retinopathy detection and classification. Traditional methods are categorized into four groups: DL, ML, hybrid DL-ML methods, and optimization-based techniques. The chapter highlights how these methods process and analyze retinal images for accurate diagnosis. It also discusses their strengths, limitations, and potential areas for improvement.
- **Chapter 3** presents a multimodal approach for the detection and early prediction of DR via ML and DL methods. Retinal images are processed and analyzed with a deep CNN, trained with optimized hyperparameters, and compared with SVM and ANN models. Experimental results show that the CNN achieves superior accuracy of 96.6% in detection and prediction. This approach demonstrates an effective and reliable method for early DR diagnosis and risk assessment.
- **Chapter 4** presents a multimodal framework combining OCT and fundus images for accurate DR detection and progression prediction. Images are denoised with Gaussian filtering and segmented using an Improved ResUNet with self-attention. Features from both modalities are fused and classified using Improved GoogLeNet with Transfer Learning, while a hybrid Bi-LSTM-SqueezeNet model predicts stage-wise progression. Experimental results show enhanced accuracy, precision, and robustness, outperforming conventional methods.
- **Chapter 5** concludes that the proposed method using OCT and fundus images with deep learning can detect and predict diabetic retinopathy accurately. It helps in early diagnosis and better patient care. The chapter also suggests future work, like using more data, adding other types of images, and improving the models for real-world use.

1.9 Summary

This chapter introduced the key concepts and motivations behind this research on DR. It begins with an overview of DR, its causes, and its impact on vision health, followed by the importance of early detection and progression prediction in preventing vision loss. The chapter then reviews different imaging modalities like fundus photography and OCT, and detection methods including manual grading, ML and DL methods. Research motivation was discussed, highlighted the need for accurate, reliable, and scalable DR detection systems. The research objectives and contributions were also presented, emphasizing the novel multimodal framework and predictive models developed to enhance early diagnosis and progression monitoring of DR.

Chapter 2
Literature Review

CHAPTER 2
LITERATURE REVIEW

2.1 Introduction

Diabetic Retinopathy (DR) has emerged as one of the important origins of preventable loss of sight worldwide mainly, amongst persons with long-term diabetes. As global diabetes occurrence continues to rise, primary recognition and precise classification of DR have become vital for active treatment and vision preservation. Medical imaging techniques such as Fundus Photography and Optical Coherence Tomography (OCT) play a central role in diagnosing DR by capturing detailed retinal structures. However, the manual interpretation of these images is highly challenging because of differences in image resolution, light settings and the subtle visual differences between disease stages. To overcome these limitations, advanced computational approaches have been progressively adopted in recent years. Machine Learning (ML) algorithms provide reliable classification through structured feature analysis, while Deep Learning (DL) models excel at automated feature extraction and large-scale data learning. Hybrid frameworks that combine ML and DL approaches further enhance model interpretability, robustness and diagnostic accuracy. Additionally, optimization-based strategies improve feature selection, hyperparameter tuning and model generalization further increases classification performance. This thesis delves into these computational strategies completely that aims to advance a novel and efficient framework for the automated classification of Diabetic Retinopathy, thereby supports timely diagnosis and improved patient outcomes.

Table 2.1 Review of Literature

Title of paper	Method Used	Findings	Limitations
[1] Automatic Diagnosis of Different Grades of Diabetic Retinopathy and Diabetic Macular Edema Using 2-D-FBSE-FAWT	2-D-FBSE-FAWT, IoT, Deep Learning	Automated diagnosis for various DR grades using advanced imaging. Integration of IoT for efficient healthcare.	Limited explanation of IoT integration impact.

[2] Internet of Things and Deep Learning Enabled Diabetic Retinopathy Diagnosis Using Retinal Fundus Images	IoT, Deep Learning	DR diagnosis with retinal fundus images using IoT. Potential of IoT in medical imaging.	Limited discussion on IoT implementation challenges.
[3] Deep Learning Techniques for Diabetic Retinopathy Classification: A Survey	Deep Learning	Survey of deep learning techniques in DR classification.	Does not provide specific findings but summarizes techniques.
[4] Explainable Diabetic Retinopathy Detection and Retinal Image Generation	Deep Learning	Emphasis on explainable DR detection in AI models.	No direct findings but highlights the importance of inter- pretability.
[5] RTNet: Relation Transformer Network for Diabetic Retinopathy Multi-Lesion Segmentation	RTNet, Deep Learning	Introduction of RTNet for multi-lesion segmentation in DR.	Limited discussion on real-world applicability.
[6] Optimizing Deep Learning Model Parameters Using Socially Implemented IoMT Systems for Diabetic Retinopathy Classification Problem	Socially Implemented IoMT, Deep Learning	Optimization of model parameters using IoMT systems.	Lack of detailed performance improvements.
[7] Robust Collaborative Learning of Patch-Level and Image-Level Annotations for Diabetic Retinopathy Grading From Fundus Image	Collaborative Learning, Deep Learning	Robust collaborative learning for enhanced DR severity classification.	Limited discussion on scalability.
[8] Multi-Stream Deep Neural Network for Diabetic Retinopathy Severity Classification Under a Boosting Framework	Multi-stream Deep Neural Networks, Deep Learning	Enhanced DR severity classification using multi-stream networks.	Doesn't address specific limitations.

[9] Vision Transformer Model for Predicting the Severity of Diabetic Retinopathy in Fundus Photography-Based Retina Images	Vision Transformer, Deep Learning	Implementation of Vision Transformer for predicting DR severity.	Limited discussion on comparative performance.
[10] DR-GAN: Conditional Generative Adversarial Network for Fine-Grained Lesion Synthesis on Diabetic Retinopathy Images	DR-GAN , Generative Adv- ersarial Networks	Introduction of DR-GAN for fine-grained lesion synthesis.	Limited discussion on practical applications.
[11] Segmentation Using the IC2T Model and Classification of Diabetic Retinopathy Using the Rock Hyrax Swarm-Based Coordination Attention Mechanism	IC2T Models, Image Segmentation	Exploration of image segmentation using IC2T models for DR.	Lack of discussion on model complexities.
[12] A Faster RCNN-Based Diabetic Retinopathy Detection Method Using Fused Features From Retina Images	Faster RCNN, Image Segmentation	DR detection with Faster RCNN-based image segmentation.	Limited discussion on real-world applications.
[13] Grading of Diabetic Retinopathy Images Based on Graph Neural Network	Graph Neural Networks, Grading DR Images	Leveraging graph neural networks for grading DR images.	Limited discussion on computational complexity.
[14] Graph Adversarial Transfer Learning for Diabetic Retinopathy Classification	Graph Neural Networks, Adv- ersarial Transfer	Utilizing graph neural networks for adversarial transfer learning in DR.	Limited discussion on transfer- ability.
[15] Uncertainty- Aware Deep Learning Methods for Robust Diabetic Retinopathy Classification	Uncertainty-Aware Deep Learning, AI Models	Focus on uncertainty-aware methods for robust DR classification.	Limited exploration of real-world uncertainty management.

[16] EDR-Net: Lightweight Deep Neural Network Architecture for Detecting Referable Diabetic Retinopathy	EDR-Net, Lightweight AI Architecture	Introduction of EDR-Net, a lightweight AI architecture for healthcare.	Limited discussion on comparative efficiency.
[17] Ensembled Deep Convolutional Generative Adversarial Network for Grading Imbalanced Diabetic Retinopathy Recognition	Ensembled Deep CNN Models, Hybrid Models	Exploration of ensembled deep CNN and hybrid models for DR recognition.	Limited discussion on the ensemble's impact.
[18] Systematic Development of AI-Enabled Diagnostic Systems for Glaucoma and Diabetic Retinopathy	AI-Enabled Diagnostic Systems	Systematic development of AI-enabled diagnostic systems in healthcare.	Doesn't provide specific findings but highlights the integration of AI.
[19] Diabetic Retinopathy Detection and Grading: A Transfer Learning Approach Using Simultaneous Parameter Optimization and Feature-Weighted ECOC Ensemble	Transfer Learning, Deep Learning	Utilization of transfer learning in DR analysis.	Limited discussion on model fine-tuning.
[20] A Hybrid Convolutional Neural Network Model for Automatic Diabetic Retinopathy Classification From Fundus Images	Hybrid CNN Models, Deep Learning	Use of hybrid CNN models for enhanced DR detection.	Limited discussion on the hybrid model's performance.
[21] Automatic Severity Classification of Diabetic Retinopathy Based on DenseNet and Convolutional Block Attention Module	DenseNet, Attention Mechanisms	Introduction of DenseNet with attention modules for DR analysis.	Limited discussion on practical implementation.
[22] Artificial Intelligence-Based Teleophthalmology Application for Diagnosis of Diabetics Retinopathy	AI-Based Teleophthalmology Applications	Advancements in AI-based teleophthalmology applications.	Limited discussion on teleophthalmology scalability.

[23] Joint Learning of Multi-Level Tasks for Diabetic Retinopathy Grading on Low-Resolution Fundus Images	Joint Learning, Low-Resolution Images	Joint learning for DR grading on low-resolution fundus images.	Limited exploration of low-resolution image challenges.

2.2 Categorization and Description of Works

In this thesis, the literature review offered in Chapter 2 classifies present Diabetic Retinopathy detection and classification approaches into three major groups: deep learning (DL)-based methods, machine learning (ML)-based methods and hybrid approaches that combine both DL and ML techniques.

2.2.1 Deep Learning based Diabetic Retinopathy Detection

In 2024, Roberto Romero-Ora′ *et al.,* [1] proposed a method that incorporated a unique attention mechanism that separately targeted dark and bright regions of the retina through a preliminary image decomposition process. This method functioned as an XAI tool that produced independent attention maps for bright and red lesions. The system also included an image quality assessment module and employed several DL strategies such as transfer learning, fine-tuning and data augmentation. The Xception structure served as the backbone for feature extraction and focal loss was utilized to mitigate the effects of class imbalance. The findings demonstrated that the framework effectively automated DR grading. The strategy of separating attention for different lesion types contributed to improved classification performance.

In 2024, Lijuan Wang conducted *et al.,* [2] researched on a group of 103 patients diagnosed with DR and admitted to the ophthalmology department between January 2023 and January 2024. Participants were randomly divided into validation and training sets in a 3:7 ratio. Two convolutional neural networks such as DenseNet and VGG19 were implemented and TL was applied. The performance of these models was evaluated against their non-transfer learning versions. The application of deep TL significantly enhanced the ability of neural networks to detect DR from OCT images. This method not only improved diagnostic accurateness but also simplified the clinical workflow for ophthalmologists that supported its broader integration into medical practice.

In 2025, El-Mehdi Chakour *et al.,* [3] introduced a portable and real-time AMD system designed for DR detection, which incorporated a refined deep learning model into a mobile-based platform. Contrasting traditional AI methods that relied on high-end computation resources and motionless fundus cameras, the proposed structure utilized a non-mydriatic retinal camera paired with a mobile device that enabled on-the-spot screening. Retinal images were enhanced through preprocessing methods such as contrast adjustment and blurring beforehand actuality evaluated by a fine-tuned DenseNet-121 model. With a typical processing time of 162.5 milliseconds, the application proved suitable for rapid assessments. Additionally, the mobile-based solution formed part of a broader tele-ophthalmology framework, which included desktop and tablet versions to support remote and accessible DR screening.

In 2024, Yovel Rom *et al.,* [4] explored a different approach that influenced artificial intelligence and machine learning to detect diabetes from retinal images even when no diabetic eye disease is present. In this work, a ML model was developed and trained using a large dataset of retinal fundus images. The patient population was categorized into groups based on how long they had been living with the condition, with each group containing individuals diagnosed within a particular time range, alongside a control group of healthy participants. The AI model demonstrated strong performance in identifying diabetes based solely on fundus imagery regardless of the presence of visible retinal damage. Its predictive capabilities were consistent across various imaging devices. These findings indicated the potential for non-invasive diabetes screening using only retinal photographs. This approach could pave the way for early detection at primary care facilities or through other accessible healthcare services, thereby helping to identify individuals with undiagnosed diabetes and improving overall health outcomes.

In 2025, María Herrero-Tudela *et al.,* [5] introduced a robust and efficient method for the automated grading of DR, with a strong emphasis on delivering interpretable visual outputs to support clinical understanding. The approach was based on a modified version of the ResNet-50 DL architecture that enhanced with several strategies such as regularization, data augmentation, TL, early stopping and fine-tuning to improve overall model performance. The model was assessed using several openly obtainable retinal image datasets and demonstrated strong and consistent results across various sources. SHAP-based visualizations revealed that changes in the retinal vasculature played a key role in DR detection. Additionally, it was observed that peripheral regions of the retina often contained initial signs of the disease that highlighted the importance of complete image analysis. This research also successfully addressed the common challenge of data imbalance that was frequently encountered in clinical environments.

In 2025, Masoud Muhammed Hassan and Halbast Rashid Ismail [6] developed a simple yet effective CNN architecture for DR classification. The same base model was then adapted using two different Bayesian strategies: one leveraged variational inference and the other utilizing Monte Carlo dropout. These adaptations allowed the model to generate posterior predictive distributions that provided insight into the confidence of its predictions. The performance of these models was assessed using well-known public datasets in the field of retinal imaging. Results from the evaluation indicated that the Bayesian-enhanced CNN models outperformed several existing approaches. Additionally, measures such as standard deviation and entropy were calculated from the predictive distributions to measure the uncertainty associated with the predictions.

In 2025, Mohsin Akram *et al.,* [8] implemented a transfer learning strategy using a DenseNet-based convolutional neural network as the foundation for diabetic retinopathy detection. Once the model was trained, Bayesian techniques were integrated to enhance its predictive reliability. Several approximation methods were explored that included Monte Carlo Dropout, Deterministic Inference and Mean Field Variational Inference that allowed for the estimation of posterior predictive distributions and offering a window into how confident the model was in its outputs. Experiments were conducted on a combined dataset of retinal images that had undergone pre-processing. The Bayesian-enhanced model consistently outperformed several conventional approaches. Alongside accuracy improvements, the use of metrics such as entropy and standard deviation provided deeper insights into the confidence levels of individual predictions. Beyond just improving classification outcomes, this study underscored the added value of Bayesian deep learning methods in medical imaging.

In 2024, Dharmalingam Muthusamy and Parimala Palani [9] developed a MAPCRCI-DMPLC model that was designed with an architecture that included an input layer, multiple hidden layers and an output layer. It aimed to distinguish diabetic retinopathy in its primary stages by delivering high accurateness with minimal computational time. The model began by accepting retinal fundus images as input from a curated dataset. In the primary hidden layer, image preprocessing was conducted using a MAP-estimated local region filtering method, which helped enhance the image quality. Another hidden layer employed Camargo's index-based

ROI extraction to locate affected areas within the retina. An experimental evaluation was conducted using a retinal image dataset, assessing various performance metrics such as image quality, detection accuracy, false detection rates, and processing time, considering both image quantity and resolution.

In 2025, Rashid Abbasi *et al.,*[10] proposed an adaptive enhancement-based DCNN model for detecting diabetic retinopathy. This model incorporated an adaptive gamma enhancement matrix aimed at optimizing color channels and standardizing distinction across images. To further improve visual quality, quantile-based histogram equalization was integrated into the model, enhancing the visibility and clarity of the fundus images particularly, those with low contrast. The enhancement method offered significant improvements in image quality, making it especially beneficial for underexposed or poorly lit retinal scans. The model's effectiveness was tested through various experiments using a well-established public dataset. It successfully classified different categories of retinal images and demonstrated a consistent improvement in visual and structural image quality. The assessment involved comparisons between original and enhanced images that revealed a noticeable increase in contrast without negotiating the structural integrity of the images.

In 2024, A. M.Mutawa *et al.,*[11] proposed the use of a CNN for detecting the different stages of DR. This study contributed to the field by implementing a novel method that incorporated two separate open datasets. This dual-dataset strategy enhanced the model's ability to generalize across previously unnoticed DR cases, as separately dataset reflected varied demographic and clinical conditions. The CNN architecture was designed to capture complex hierarchical features within retinal images using asymmetric weight distributions. Prior to training, all images underwent preprocessing by means of contrast-limited adaptive histogram compensation alongside discrete wavelet transforms to improve feature extraction and image quality. Among the tested configurations, the CNN model qualified with the Adam optimizer demonstrated promising results in both precision and diagnostic capability.

In 2024, AmarShukla *et al.*,[12] developed a hybrid model called HybridFusionNet that combined the capabilities of ViT with attention mechanisms to enhance diagnostic performance. The proposed method was considered to improve classification outcomes in both binary and multi-class stages by leveraging deep features extracted from different stages of DR progression. The HybridFusionNet model demonstrated notable improvements in both the multi-class and binary stages that showcased its effectiveness in achieving higher diagnostic accuracy.

In 2022, Al-Omaisi *et al.*,[13] applied deep learning techniques, specifically a CNN, to analyze retinal fundus images and identify the different stages of DR. The dataset was extensive but had some limitations, such as being unbalanced with a small number of labeled images. To overcome these issues, the study introduced regularization, preprocessing and augmentation techniques to enhance the dataset that made it more suitable for training the model and improved overall performance. Among these models, ResNet-101 delivered the highest accuracy and exhibited the best performance with notably low training and testing losses. It was subsequently evaluated on images from additional databases as well.

In 2025, Amira J. Zaylaa and Sylva Kourtian [14] focused on utilizing various pre-trained DNNs and statistical metrics to create an automated framework for detecting DR in optical images. And employed ROC to evaluate the performance of individual network. Real and morally gained datasets were used to authenticate and strengthen the robustness of the proposed recognition system. The outcomes indicated that, in terms of general performance in DR detection, ResNet-50 emerged as the top-performing model, followed closely by GoogleNet, both achieved high sensitivity. In terms of precision, the models were quite similar. These outcomes highlighted the possible of the automatic DR detection and diagnosis framework as a valuable tool to support doctors in making early diagnoses that saved both time and effort. Moving forward, future improvements could include the growth of a grading algorithm and the exploration of additional strategies to enhance the diagnosis of DR and automatic detection with a view to integrate the system into digital slit lamp machines for wider clinical application.

In 2020, K. Shankar *et al.,*[15] introduced a novel automated model called HPTI-v4, designed to detect and classify DR from color fundus images. Throughout the preprocessing stage, the divergence of the fundus images was improved using a CLAHE method. Following this, the images were segmented using a histogram-based segmentation approach. The HPTI-v4 model was then employed to abstract vital features from the segmented images, which were subsequently classified using an MLP.

In 2024, Ma Yinghua *et al.,*[16] introduced a modified U-Net deep learning model specifically designed to segment hard exudates effectively even with limited data. The system was tested and trained on a small set of original retinal images, which supplemented by image augmentation to improve its robustness. Despite the constraints of the dataset, the modified U-Net achieved high sensitivity, precision, specificity and accuracy that resulted in a notably high F1 score. These conclusions highlighted the possiblity of the proposed method to advance DR diagnosis, even with limited resources. By adapting existing deep learning models, the study demonstrated significant improvements in diagnostic accuracy for DR. However, further validation with larger datasets and comparisons with other methods were necessary to fully confirm the results. This research contributed to the enhanced detection of hard exudates in DR, which could ultimately lead to improved outcomes for patients.

In 2023, Ghadah Alwakid *et al.,*[17] introduced a DL model to diagnose all five stages of DR with greater accuracy than previous methods. The approach consisted of two scenarios: the first incorporated image enhancement through a CLAHE filtering algorithm combined with an ESRGAN, while in second scenario image enhancement was not applied. Augmentation techniques were employed to generate a stable dataset that ensured that both scenarios used the same parameters. The advanced system was verified on the APTOS datasets, utilized the Inception-V3 architecture. The results revealed that the model with image enhancement achieved significantly higher accuracy compared to the non-enhanced scenario that surpassed current approaches for detection of the 5 phases of DR.

In 2025, Bambang Krismono Triwijoyo *et al.,*[18] utilized secondary data, specifically retinal images from the open-source Messidor database, which contained a collection of retinal images. The dataset was divided into a validation set and a training set. The image examination procedure involved segmenting retinal blood vessels using the Otsu segmentation algorithm. A structural method was then employed to extract detailed features of the blood vessels around the OD. This step also included analyzing the assessment between the AVR width. The study applied a DCNN model for classification, with cross-justification performed using the Leave-One-Out method. Key findings from this research included the implementation of the AVR computation algorithm, which helped create a novel dataset with multiple classification groups. Additionally, the architectural conditions of the CNN model were refined by determining the appropriate input size, number of nodes, layer depth, learning rate, transfer functions and the number of epochs through careful hyperparameter tuning.

In 2025, Kerem GENCER *et al.,*[19] proposed a novel framework that integrated GANs for data augmentation, denoising autoencoders for noise reduction and transfer learning with EfficientNetB0 to enhance the performance of DR classification models. GANs were used to produce high-quality artificial retinal images that addressed the issue of enriching the training and class imbalance of dataset. To advance the quality of these images further, denoising autoencoders were applied to reduce noise and eliminate common artifacts such as motion blur, speckle noise and illumination inconsistencies. This resulted in reliable and clean images that could be fed into the system model for classification. EfficientNetB0 was then modified on this denoised and augmented dataset. This study underscored the transformative potential of DL in overcoming key tasks in the diagnosis of DR.

In 2025, Sebastian Dinesen *et al.,*[20] utilized six-field retinal images classified at level 4 on the International Clinical Diabetic Retinopathy Disease Severity Scale, which were collected as part of the Danish screening program for diabetic retinopathy from a region in Denmark between 2009 and 2019. A expert grader physically characterized the images into inactive or active PDR that was followed by reassessment from two self-regulating expert graders. In cases of difference, the last classification was completed through partnership between the initial grader and one of the minor graders. A total of images was classified as active PDR. A pre-established DL segmentation model was applied to explain nine different lesion types. The segmentations for new vessels and preretinal hemorrhages were adjusted for accuracy before training the DL algorithm. After segmentation and classification, the dataset was divided into validation, training and testing sets. The testing set was supplemented with additional images of inactive PDR.

In 2024, Lakshay Arora *et al.,*[21] introduced an innovative deep learning framework designed for the diagnosis of DR. The system utilized the EfficientNetB0 architecture to categorize the severity of DR from retinal images. Through influencing progressive computer vision and ML techniques, the system aimed to provide accurate and reliable diagnoses of DR. Nonstop experimentation and testing demonstrated the effectiveness of this structure that showed capable results that could transform both the diagnosis and treatment of DR. These conclusions underscored the possibility of the proposed framework to significantly advance DR diagnosis. With access to more progressive datasets and greater exercise resources, it could provide clinicians with a influential tool for initial interference that ultimately improved patient outcomes.

In 2025, Mishmala Sushith *et al.,*[22] introduced a novel hybrid deep learning framework that combined CNNs with RNNs for the early detection and monitoring of DR progression using retinal fundus images. By leveraging the progressive nature of disease development, the proposed approach integrated temporal material across multiple retinal scans, which enhanced the system's detection precision. The framework was evaluated using openly obtainable diabetic retinopathy datasets from DRIVE and Kaggle, which offered a wide range of marked retinal images. The hybrid model used a CNN to abstract retinal images spatial features. To seizure both broader patterns and fine details, the spatial feature extraction process was improved by multi-scale feature extraction. These refined spatial features were then processed through an RNN with an attention mechanism that allowed the model to seizure temporal dependances and consider the most relevant aspects of the data for examination.

In 2023, Abdul Rahaman Wahab Sait *et al.,*[25] developed a lightweight DL-based system for grading DR severity that would function effectively even with limited computational resources. The proposed framework incorporated an image pre-processing method to mitigate artifacts and noise commonly originated in fundus images. The extraction of feature procedure utilized the Yolo V7 technique to generate feature sets. To optimize the selection of relevant features, a customized QMPA was employed. For forecasting the harshness levels of DR, the framework used a hyperparameter-optimized MobileNet V3 architecture. The lightweight nature of the framework made it particularly appropriate for healthcare settings, especially in remote areas with limited resources. The proposed system could potentially be applied as a mobile application to assist clinicians in treating and diagnosing DR patients. In the future, the author aimed to add improvement the model's competence particularly, in detecting DR from low-quality fundus images.

In 2025, S Jahangeer Sidiq *et al.,*[29] proposed a deep learning-based ensemble approach that utilized both pre-trained and customized bi-class as base learners. Models such as MobileNet, InceptionV3, and DenseNet121 were selected due to their robust performance in ensemble learning tasks. Unlike previous studies that treated DR detection as a solo complex multi-class problem or grouped the early stages together as one class (0 to 3) while treating the severe stage as another class (4), this approach divided the task into numerous simpler two-class problems using the OVO strategy. The study also incorporated data augmentation techniques to improve model performance. The evaluation was based on metrics such as precision, recall, F1-score, and accuracy, with the ensemble models showing outstanding performance across most of the datasets. Additionally, these models required fewer trainable parameters that made them a extremely efficient choice for DR detection.

In 2025, Sreebhadra Vallukappully *et al.,*[34] proposed a novel transfer learning approach utilizing NASNet-Large and ResNet-50 convolutional neural networks. Various image pre-processing techniques were verified in combination to optimize performance. To address oversampling, class imbalance and data augmentation were employed, which ensured reliable performance metrics. The models demonstrated strong detection capabilities when evaluated on a typical dataset of expert-labelled DR fundus images. The best-performing frameworks attained impressive precision when organizing unseen images that showed exceptional results for detecting early-stage DR and multi-stage DR classification. The study emphasized the efficiency of combining transfer learning with advanced DL models and traditional image processing techniques for accurate classification and DR detection.

In 2025, Hongkang Wu built *et al.,*[36] developed and validated an AI-driven system called DRAMA, which was designed to diagnose diabetic retinopathy (DR) across diverse and heterogeneous datasets. The aim was to improve diagnostic precision and effectiveness. The AI framework was developed using EfficientNet-B2 that was pre-trained on the ImageNet dataset. It was designed to perform 11 multi-label tasks such as quality assessment, image type identification, DME detection and lesion detection. The system utilized AdamP optimizer and the LabelSmoothingCrossEntropy to improve its sturdiness and convergence. The model's performance was evaluated using metrics such as precision, specificity, AUC and sensitivity. External validation was carried out using datasets from various medical centers.

In 2025, Saad Alanazi and Rayan Alanazi [39] proposed a comprehensive solution for DR detection using deep learning algorithms. To address class imbalance and enhance the model's performance, the SMOTE was initially applied for the data balance. Additionally, Weiner and median filtering techniques were employed to reduce noise in retinal images and enhance image quality for further analysis. The VGG model, originally designed for classification and segmentation tasks, was leveraged for its capability to capture fine visual details. The extracted features were then integrated into several CNN models, which identified distinctive patterns to evaluate the severity of DR. Federated learning was incorporated into the system, allowing collaborative training across multiple medical institutions while ensuring patient privacy and security. The mixture of data preprocessing with SMOTE, image filtering, VGG-based feature extraction and FedCNN produced promising results that demonstrated the potential for secure and scalable DR detection systems. This approach highlighted the effectiveness of VGG for feature extraction and the value of federated learning in maintaining data security across institutions.

In 2024, Akshit Aggarwal *et al.,*[40] introduced a specialized computational framework named DRCNN for the purpose of detecting DR. This system evaluated retina scans from potentially affected individuals by contrasting them with those from healthy eyes. The architecture incorporated essential CNN components such as pooling layers, convolutional layers, flattening, fully connected layers and dropout for feature extraction and interpretation. For model optimization and improved accuracy, a pre-trained deep learning architecture was utilized, alongside an advanced optimization algorithm for efficient training. The model was tested using various portions of the dataset for training and evaluation to determine its effectiveness under different conditions. Results demonstrated that the proposed model performs most effectively when a larger share of the dataset is dedicated to training. With millions of parameters, the model was capable of achieving high classification accuracy and was also validated using separate datasets to ensure reliability.

In 2024, Mustafa Youldash *et al.,*[43] utilized AI technology that focused on deep learning, to achieve two main goals: to perform binary classification to determine whether a patient had DR and to conduct multi-class classification to accurately identify the stage of DR in a timely manner. The proposed model employed six pre-trained CNN. The study was carried out in two phases. The outcomes presented that the RegNetX080 model achieved high accuracy in binary classification, while EfficientNetB3 achieved well in multi-class sorting. These findings demonstrated the possibility of AI for the initial and precise classification and detection of DR. The paper highlighted the potential impact of AI on improving healthcare systems and clinical decision-making, contributing to the early detection of DR in Saudi Arabia.

In 2023, Ghadah Alwakid *et al.,*[44] aimed to identify DR and its stages using retinal scans from the —APTOS 2019 Blindness Detection‖ dataset, employing a DL model that incorporated multiple scenarios. The study utilized data augmentation techniques to create a complete dataset, ensuring consistent hyperparameters across all test cases. A CNN model was then employed for classification, with various image enhancement techniques applied to improve visual quality. In addition to these results, the APTOS 2019 dataset was used to develop calculation metrics that includes recall, precision and F1-score, to assess the effectiveness of the proposed model. This approach was found to be more efficient in detecting DR locations compared to both conventional DL models and other state-of-the-art technologies.

In 2024, M. S. Santos *et al.,*[45] introduced a novel approach using a SCNN for predicting DR, designed to be used by primary care professionals. The SCNN analyzed sets of eye fundus images and uses shared weights in its coatings to extract key features, which allowed the model to quantity the similarity between the productions of the neural network. Despite dealing with the limitations of small and imbalanced datasets, the SCNN demonstrated promising results. The model reliability outdone other methods particularly, in terms of recall performance. These results suggest that DL techniques particularly, those utilized Siamese networks could serve as a practical and effective tool for DR screening.

In 2023, Mohammad B. Khan *et al.,*[46] compared two deep learning architectures, Inception v3 and DenseNet-121 that used datasets of original color images and segmented retinal vessel images. The results demonstrated that both models attained high precision with the original images, whereas the segmented vessel images yielded substantially lower accuracy. These findings indicated that using segmented retinal blood vessels added limited value, and that original color fundus images were more effective for DL-based diagnosis of DR.

In 2022, Usharani Bhimavarapu and Gopi Battineni [47] introduced an improved activation function for diagnosing DR from fundus images, which effectively reduced both the loss and processing time. The model was trained and tested using several datasets, including DRIVE, DIARETDB0, Kaggle and CHASE. Among the diverse CNN models evaluated, the ResNet-152 model achieved the highest precision with the Kaggle dataset. The improved activation function demonstrated strong potential for diagnosing DR from retinal fundus images.

In 2025, Udayaraju Pamula *et al.,*[48] proposed a novel approach for early DR detection by integrating advanced machine learning techniques. The framework followed a three-phase methodology: primary image preprocessing, HNN blood vessel segmentation and AM-CapsuleNet feature extraction. Extracted features were optimized using a Taylor-based AVOA and classified with a BCAN. To further improve classification accuracy, a hybrid EFAOA was employed to refine the exploration phase that ensured faster convergence. The framework was assessed on a balanced dataset from the APTOS 2019 Blindness Detection test that demonstrated higher performance in both precision and effectiveness. The findings indicated that the proposed framework provided a robust solution for early DR classification and detection, which possibly enabled timely and precise diagnosis to improve patient outcomes.

In 2022, Posham Uppamma *et al.,*[49] focused on predicting DR that is a chronic eye disease caused by diabetes that can lead to blindness. Early diagnosis was critical to reduce the risk of vision loss. Feature selection and hyperparameter tuning were conducted using the TAVO algorithm and the most significant features were then input into a SqueezeNet classifier to predict the occurrence of DR. The prediction results were stored within a blockchain framework, which was retrieved by an EHR director to ensure authorized access to patient data and predictions.

In 2022, Ghada Atteia *et al.,*[50] explored the benefits of using the BO algorithm to improve the classification performance of deep learning networks in detecting DM from retinal images. Two new custom CNN models were proposed for DM detection in two different types of retinal photography: fundus retinography and OCT. The Bayesian optimization approach was used to regulate the optimal structures for the CNN models and to fine-tune their hyperparameters. The results of the paper confirmed that Bayesian optimization played a significant role in enhancing the performance of the proposed CNN models for classifying diabetic maculopathy in both OCT and fundus images.

In 2022, Bassam A. Y. Alqaralleh *et al.,*[51] introduces an ODL-FDRDC method. The primary goal of the proposed ODL-FDRDC approach is to detect DR and classify its various stages using retinal fundus images. The method incorporates a region-growing segmentation technique to accurately identify infected areas. For feature extraction, it employs a fusion of two deep learning models such that MobileNet and CapsNet, whose performance is further optimized through hyperparameter tuning using the COA. Additionally, a GRU is utilized for effective DR classification.

In 2024, V Thanikachalam *et al.,*[52] proposes an automatic DR/DME grade detection approach using advanced image processing techniques. Firstly, the input retinal fundus images are pre-processed with DWT to improve visual quality. Accurate detection of DR/DME is further facilitated using an ANN-based segmentation method. Following segmentation, features are extracted using the AGF, known for its excellent retinal vein detection capability, and refined using RF for feature selection, leveraging its strong generalization power. The RF technique also helps recover the classification performance of a DCNN.

In 2022, Anas Bilal *et al.,*[53] proposed a novel two-stage approach for the automated classification of DR. To tackle the challenge posed by the low prevalence of positive instances in the detection of the asymmetric OD and BV, where preprocessing and data augmentation techniques were utilized to improve both the quality and quantity of the images. The first stage involved the use of two independent U-Net models for the segmentation of BV and OD. The additional stage employed a symmetric hybrid CNN-SVD model, which was developed after preprocessing to extract and select the furthermost discriminative features following BV and OD extraction. The model utilized Inception-V3 based on TL and identified DR by recognizing retinal biomarkers such as hemorrhages, microaneurysms and exudates.

In 2024, Chaichana Suedumrong *et al.,*[54] used CNNs to classify the severity of DR using retinal images from the EyePACS dataset, which contained a large number of images categorized into multiple stages. While prior research often focused on simplifying DR diagnosis by classifying the condition into just two categories such as no DR and changing levels of DR, this approach took a different route. Rather than reducing the number of stages, they employed a smaller and more flexible CNN structure, which enabled more thorough classification into five distinct stages of DR. To improve the model's performance, they have implemented several image preprocessing techniques, such as background removal, grayscale conversion and data augmentation. Notably, we found that removing the background significantly improved the model's performance, leading to a notable increase in validation accuracy. This study highlighted the position of advanced data preprocessing in medical image analysis and demonstrated how it can help advance the precision of automated DR diagnosis.

In 2025, Qing Yang *et al.,*[55] proposed a novel deep learning framework that combined depthwise separable convolution with a MVAM for efficient DR diagnosis using retinal images. The model incorporated multi-scale feature fusion through parallel convolutions, which allowed it to seizure lesions of various sizes. Additionally, Gabor filters were employed to develop vascular texture and improve lesion detection, particularly for initial structural abnormalities, all while reducing computational costs. The framework was evaluated on both the DR and ocular disease datasets. Results showed that the proposed method attained superior performance, with significantly higher precision compared to traditional models like CNN_eye, VGG, and U-Net. Furthermore, the training time for the proposed approach was notably shorter than that of U-Net and VGG, demonstrating its potential for practical use in clinical DR screening.

In 2023, Cheena Mohanty *et al.,*[57] addressed class imbalance in available datasets typically hampers the performance of these models. This study presented a modified DL approach that integrated GANs with AlexNet to address dataset imbalance and optimize classification. The framework was designed to classify DR severity into five categories: proliferative DR mild, asymptomatic and severe non-proliferative DR, moderate. The experimental outcomes showed that the GAN-AlexNet model outperformed the standard AlexNet in terms of accuracy, precision, recall and F1-score.

In 2023, Awais Bajwa *et al.,*[58] developed a deep learning model and trained on a private dataset and its performance was evaluated in real-time at the

SIOVS. The model first assessed the quality of the test images and then classified them as either DR-positive or DR-negative. The results were further reviewed by clinical experts to validate the model's performance. The study screened a large number of patients over several weeks and the model demonstrated high sensitivity, specificity and accuracy in detection of DR that showed its possibility as a dependable tool for primary diagnosis.

In 2025, Dileep Kumar Agarwal1 and Maninder Singh Nehra [59] addressed key challenges in DR detection such as noise, poor image quality and variability in disease presentation, using a two-phase experimental approach. In the primary phase, CNN models were applied but showed limited performance due to overfitting and basic preprocessing, which affected generalization. In the second phase, these issues were addressed through advanced preprocessing techniques that included contrast enhancement using CLAHE, and data augmentation combined with regularization methods such as L2 regularization and dropout. This work demonstrates that combining sophisticated preprocessing with ensemble learning can create efficient and reliable DR detection systems, which are particularly useful in clinical and resource-limited settings for early diagnosis and intervention.

In 2024, Xuebin Xu *et al.,*[60] proposed a multi-view joint learning model called RT2Net for DR diagnosis. The model combines total features from fundus images with local detailed features from vascular images that overcame the restrictions of relying on a single image type. The process begins with preprocessing the original image using techniques such as contrast enhancement and segmenting the vascular structure. Both the vascular and fundus images are then processed through separate branches of RT2Net for feature fusion and a feature extraction module combines the outputs. Finally, an optimized classification model identifies the severity of DR.

In 2023, Usharani Bhimavarapu *et al.,*[62] proposes an enhanced CNN model for automatic DR detection from fundus images. The model incorporates an enhanced pooling function united with an activation function in a ResNet-50 architecture. The pooling function enlarges the receptive field of the convolutional layers that reduced the resolution of feature maps and lowered computational complexity and memory requirements while retaining important image features. This approach allowed for efficient lesion detection with reduced processing time and minimal loss. The enhanced ResNet-50 model was tested and trained on multiple retinal image datasets, demonstrating higher accuracy than previous state-of-the-art methods. The results confirmed that the introduced model is highly effective for automated DR diagnosis and could suggestively support clinical decision-making.

In 2023, V. Banupriya and S. Anusuya [63] aimed to enhance the diagnosis of diabetic retinopathy by developing an EDLM designed for more accurate and timely identification of DR compared to existing CNN-based models. The presented framework was intended to distinguish a range of lesions in retinal images at initial stages. Initially, features were extracted from the retinal fundus images and input into the EDLM classification model. To address dimensionality, EDLM was applied. Furthermore, the classification and feature extraction processes were done using the SGD optimizer.

In 2025, N. Mohana Suganthi and M. Arun [64] proposed a novel framework using CCNN for the detection of DR. Initially, RFI underwent noise reduction through the WIR algorithm to eliminate noise artifacts. Following this, the CCNN model was employed to categorize the images into abnormal and normal categories. To further improve the model's performance, the SSO algorithm was utilized. The proposed method achieved impressive performance, significantly outperforming established CNN-based models. The Curvelet CNN approach demonstrated a substantial improvement in classification accuracy, Triple-DRNet, superior DenseNet 121 and EfficientNetB4 by notable margins.

In 2025, Nouf Al-Kahtani *et al.,* [65] introduced a novel method, the DMBOTL-MRDD, aimed at detecting and classifying multiple retinal diseases based on fundus images. The DMBOTL-MRDD method utilized WF for noise reduction in the images. ShuffleNetv2, a lightweight CNN was employed for extracting feature vectors from the retinal images. To optimize the hyperparameters of the ShuffleNetv2 model, the DMBO was applied. Additionally, the method incorporated a ML-AE for detecting multiple retinal diseases that included diabetic retinopathy, age-related macular degeneration and glaucoma. The DMBOTL-MRDD approach was evaluated using a benchmark fundus imaging dataset. Investigational outcomes established that the presented technique outdone current methods and achieved a notably higher accuracy in classifying retinal diseases.

In 2023, Heba M. El-Hoseny *et al.,* [66] distinguish between different stages of diabetes and assess the model's ability to differentiate between them. The performance of the model was assessed using several metrics such as accuracy, AUC, recall and precision. The researchers employed various techniques, including data cleansing, TL and CNN to efficiently detect and categorize the diseases associated with DR. They utilized the VGG-16 CNN model, incorporating advanced parameters to boost its performance and robustness. The results of this model outperformed those achieved by the AE filter, which demonstrated a high level of accuracy. This study underscored the importance of optimizing deep TL for enhancing the classification metrics of diabetic retinopathy across its various stages.

In 2024, Chunjuan Huang *et al.,* [67] proposed to enhance the detection of diabetic retinopathy by improving diagnostic accuracy and identifying cases in their early stages. The approach combined the MobileNet-V2 DL model with the to optimize feature selection, which is essential for recognizing abnormalities and patterns associated with diabetic retinopathy. The Diabetic Retinopathy 2015 dataset was used to evaluate the performance of the MobileNet-V2/IFHO model. The results showed that the MobileNet-V2/IFHO model steadily outperformed other approaches in terms of key performance indicators such as precision, accuracy and recall. Additionally, it established higher performance when equated to advanced techniques, excelling in specificity, F1 score and AUC. These findings highlighted the potential of the MobileNet-V2/IFHO model as a valuable tool for refining the diagnosis of diabetic retinopathy. However, further authentication and challenging on larger datasets were recommended to confirm the model's efficiency and sturdiness in real-world clinical applications.

In 2025, Tariq Mahmood *et al.,* [68] addressed the lack of dual-modal data and effective feature fusion methods hinder their full potential, particularly due to multi-scale variations. This study tackles these challenges by concentrating on multi-scale retinal vessel segmentation, attention-based grading, data augmentation and dual feature fusion. The presented framework seeks to advance complete segmentation for retinal images with thicknesses varying vessel. It utilizes a dual-branch parallel architecture that mixes a transformer encoder with a CNN encoder to capture both global and local data for synergistic saliency learning. Additionally, the framework integrates attention modules and residual structures to identify critical lesions, thereby enhancing the accuracy and reliability of DR grading.

In 2025, Jyotirmayee Rautaray *et al.,* [69] introduced FastEffNet, an innovative framework that utilizes transformer-based KD to improve DR severity classification while minimizing computational complexity. The approach employed FastViT-MA26 as the teacher model and EfficientNet-B0 as the student model that achieved an optimal balance between exactness and computational efficiency. The research used the APTOS blindness recognition dataset, which included images across various severity levels. The dataset was pre-processed, split, normalized and augmented to address the issue of class imbalance. The trainer model was trained and validated before moving its knowledge to the apprentice model that enabled the apprentice to replicate the trainer's performance while keeping a lightweight architecture. Among all the student models, EfficientNet-B0 demonstrated the highest classification precision, F1-score, accuracy and recall, along with impressive values for CKS, WKS, MCC and AUC, while maintaining a low KD loss. Additionally, it achieved a relatively low computational cost that made it an effective, optimized lightweight model for DR detection. These results highlighted the potential of KD-based lightweight models in delivering high diagnostic accuracy while reducing computational overhead, thus facilitated cost-effective and scalable solutions for DR screening.

In 2025, Yuanyuan Liu *et al.,* [70] proposed a model called the STMF-DRNet. The model employed the Swin-TransformerV2 combined with a hybrid attention mechanism as the backbone to extract key lesion features from the images.

To improve the integration of features at various scales, a multi-branch cascading method was applied that optimized the retention of lesion-specific data and enhanced the precision of classification. Furthermore, category attention mechanisms were utilized to highlight more distinct regional features in the fundus images that improved the network's ability to detect lesions. When evaluated on multiple datasets such that DDR, EyePACS, APTOS-2019 and a clinical dataset, STMF-DRNet demonstrated strong performance particularly, on clinical data. The model showed significant improvements in accuracy, specificity, recall, F1-Score and Kappa. These results underscored the potential of STMF-DRNet in advancing DR diagnosis, particularly in challenging clinical environments.

2.2.2 Machine Learning based Diabetic Retinopathy Detection

In 2025, Cui Xuehao *et al.,* [28] develop predictive models using ML techniques to enhance early detection and risk assessment for DR. Immunometabolic indices associated with insulin resistance, inflammation, and lipid metabolism were evaluated. Multivariate logistic regression models were used to explore the relations with DR, while Bayesian kernel machine regression was employed to analyze nonlinear interactions among the variables. Eight different ML models that included ensemble methods were developed to predict the risk of DR. Feature importance was assessed using SHAP. The use of ML models proved effective in identifying individuals at high risk that highlighted their potential utility in clinical settings for targeted preventive care and early DR detection.

In 2025, Krishnendu Barik and Anil Kumar [30] proposed novel diagnostic biomarkers for DR by analyzing DEGs in peripheral blood samples from DR patients and healthy controls using RNA sequencing. Additionally, investigation of immune cell infiltration revealed a significant link between these genes particularly, DRAXIN and the immune microenvironment that suggested a role in modifiable immune responses in DR. These findings highlighted the potential of these genes as biomarkers for DR detection and offered new insights into disease mechanisms that paved the way for targeted therapeutic strategies.

In 2024, Xu Wang *et al.,* [31] develop a risk prediction model for DR by integrating machine learning techniques with SHAP. The study began with data preprocessing, addressing misplaced outliers and values, and selecting relevant features through information gain. A prediction model was then built using the CatBoost algorithm, with the results of the model being interpreted through SHAP analysis. The study concluded that monitoring and effectively managing certain indices, such as kidney function and blood sugar levels, could help prevent diabetic retinopathy. Additionally, the investigation into the relationships between various factors provided deeper insights into potential risk factors, offering valuable perspectives for initial inhibition and clinical diagnosis of DR.

In 2025, Wassila Saiah *et al.,* [32] explored four novel iminocoumarin derivatives, which had been previously synthesized and characterized, for their antioxidant, anti-inflammatory, and antidiabetic effects across various concentrations. The research utilized ANN methods and RSM in a two-variable process involving the iminocoumarins and their concentrations to assess the compounds' impact on various monitored parameters. The results demonstrated that the antioxidant action of the composites was evaluated using the DPPH scavenging assay, where they showed significant DPPH inhibitory effects, with IC_{50} values spanning a specific range. The study suggested that these synthesized iminocoumarin derivatives hold potential as effective agents for the development of anti-inflammatory, antioxidants and antidiabetic compounds.

In 2025, Ashim Chakraborty *et al.,* [35] presented a reliable approach for detecting the early stages of DR from fundus images. A relative examination was conducted between a supervised ML algorithm and physical classification performed by trained optometrists to appraise the method. The findings demonstrated the efficiency of the decision-based system for early DR detection that highlighted its potential for deployment in portable screening systems that could serve populations in remote or underserved regions.

In 2024, Carolyn Yu Tung Wong *et al.,* [38] developed AutoML model using CFPs from a publicly available dataset containing thousands of labeled images. These images were first studied for quality before being uploaded to the Google Cloud Vertex AI platform for training and testing. A multi-class classification model was trained to distinguish CRVO, DR and BRVO from normal retinal images. The model was validated with an external dataset consisting of additional CFPs. Various performance metrics such as AUROC and sensitivity, were evaluated. The performance of the AutoML model was then compared with the best existing DL-based models for DR and RVO classification identified through a literature review.

2.2.3 Hybrid model based Diabetic Retinopathy Detection

In 2024, Ayesha Jabbar *et al.,* [7] introduced an advanced deep transfer learning-based system designed for real-time DR detection using fundus cameras. The goal of this PAPER was to advance a well-organized and appropriate support system to help DR patients better accomplish their health. The presented system utilized fundus imaging to capture retinal images, which were then sent to a processing unit for accurate disease harshness classification and detection. Detailed information was generated to guide the next steps in medical treatment based on the identified stage of DR. By employing deep transfer learning algorithms particularly, VGGNet, the system enabled real-time DR detection. The performance of the system was systematically evaluated and compared to existing research outcomes.

In 2022, Muhammad Mohsin Butt *et al.,* [23] proposed a hybrid approach for detecting and classifying Diabetic Retinopathy in retinal fundus images. TL was applied to pre-trained CNN models to extract relevant features. These features were then combined to create a hybrid feature vector, which was fed into numerous classifiers for both multiclass and binary classification of fundus images. The performance of the framework was evaluated using several metrics and the results were compared to other recent methods for DR detection. The proposed technique demonstrated an important development in DR detection for retinal images. For binary classification, the modified approach attained a high level of accuracy, while it also performed well in multiclass classification that highlighted its effectiveness in identifying different stages of DR.

In 2024, Kinza Nazir *et al.,* [24] employed a weighted average ensemble approach, combining three deep learning models: Inception-v3, VGG16, and a custom convolutional neural network. This approach yielded impressive results, outperforming other pre-trained models. It achieved high accuracy, F1 score, precision, recall and AUC, demonstrating its efficiency and potential as a clinical assistant for detecting and grading diabetic retinopathy. A thorough comparative analysis further emphasized the efficiency of the presented model in providing dependable results.

In 2024, Intifa Aman Taifa *et al.,* [26] introduced a novel approach to DR detection by combining machine learning algorithms with deep feature extraction techniques. The hybrid model demonstrated high exactness in both multi-class and binary classification tasks, with DenseNet121 showing the best performance among the feature extractors. The results indicated that this hybrid approach was effective for early detection of diabetic retinopathy, offering significant potential for improving medical intervention and patient outcomes.

In 2025, Bishamber Nath *et al.,* [27] focused on analyzing twenty-seven clinical and biochemical characteristics from 188 individuals, divided into four groups: HC, T2DM, NPDR, and PDR. Several ML models were used to examine the data and SHAP was applied to the most effective RF model to determine the clinical relevance of the identified features. Additionally, CNN and GNN were utilized to classify DR based on fundus images. In conclusion, the random forest model successfully identified DR risk factors in the Northeast Indian population, while the GNN established robust performance in classification of image. The integration of ML and deep learning methods contributed to enhanced early risk assessment and diagnosis of DR, thereby improved disease management and patient outcomes.

In 2025, Pooja Bidwai Sidiq *et al.,*[33] proposed a new model called the DE-ExLNN. This model integrated an explainable CNN with a LightGBM that achived highly precise results in DR detection. In this framework, LightGBM served as the core detection model, while the explainable CNN helped address challenges that conventional CNN classifiers could not resolute. A convention dataset specifically, formed for this study included both OCTA and fundus images collected from real-time environments. This dataset outperformed traditional DR datasets in providing more accurate results.

In 2024, Atta Rahman *et al.,*[37] employed three promising machine learning models: SVM, KNN and HGB. Feature selection was performed through transfer learning on retinal fundus images from the APTOS dataset, which originally included multiple categories of DR but was simplified to a binary classification of No DR and DR. The results showed that the SVM model outperformed the other approaches, achieving superior accuracy when compared to preceding studies using the same dataset. This approach, which was evaluated by medical professionals, presents a appreciated solution for the early detection of DR and could help as an effective clinical decision support system.

In 2023, Cheena Mohanty *et al.,*[41] used retinal images from the APTOS 2019 Blindness Detection Kaggle Dataset, which suffered from an imbalanced class distribution. This issue was addressed using appropriate balancing techniques during preprocessing. The model's performance was evaluated based on accuracy, with the results showed that the hybrid network achieved a notable level of accuracy, while the DenseNet 121 model outperformed it with significantly higher accuracy. A relative examination with other approaches using the similar dataset also highlighted the higher performance of DenseNet 121. The findings underscored the potential of deep learning models in the classification and early detection of DR. The DenseNet 121 model in particular, demonstrated strong effectiveness in this area. The employment of such automated approaches could greatly enhance the competence and precision of DR diagnosis that offered significant benefits for both health care providers and patients.

In 2023, Uzair Ishtiaq *et al.,*[42] introduced a method for detecting and classifying the stages of DR, focusing on distinguishing between non-proliferative and proliferative stages. The proposed classification approach was built on a hybrid method that combined image preprocessing and ensemble features. A CNN was developed from scratch for this research. By merging LBP with deep learning features, an ensemble feature vector was created. This vector was then optimized using the SCA and the BDA. The optimized feature vector was input into various machine learning classifiers, with the SVM classifier achieving the maximum classification precision on a openly available dataset (Kaggle EyePACS). Extensive testing and assessments with existing state-of-the-art methods demonstrated the effectiveness of the presented approach.

In 2023, Ahlam Shamsan *et al.,*[43] developed three approaches, each comprising two systems, for the early detection of DR progression. All color fundus images underwent image enhancement and contrast adjustment to emphasize regions of interest. Features extracted using DenseNet-121 and AlexNet were then processed with PCA to hand-picked the most relevant features and reduce dimensionality. The first approach involves analyzing DR images for early prediction using an ANN trained on the low-dimensional features obtained from DenseNet-121 and AlexNet. The second approach integrates the important low-dimensional features from both models before and after PCA for DR image analysis. The third approach combines radiomic features, which consist of CNN-derived features from DenseNet-121 and AlexNet along with handcrafted features extracted using methods such as DWT, LBP, FCH and GLCM for early prediction via ANN.

In 2023, Yusuf Bahri Özçelik and Aytaç Altan [61] presents a robust AI model designed to classify the stages of DR from fundus images with high accuracy and low computational cost, while addressing the nonlinear dynamics present in the data. The model operates through four main stages, following preprocessing. During preprocessing, fractal analysis is used to examine chaotic patterns in the dataset of fundus images. The framework was verified on a dataset covering all DR stages, from no DR to proliferative DR, and its robustness was validated through cross-validation. Comparisons with traditional machine learning methods, such as support vector machines, showed that the proposed model efficiently overcomes nonlinear dynamics and delivers reliable and precise diagnosis for all stages of DR.

2.3 Research Gaps and Challenges

Gaps:

- Most studies use minor or single-center datasets that limits the generalization to diverse populations.
- Existing models often fail to combine data from various sources like fundus images and clinical features (e.g., blood sugar levels, age).
- Many models struggle to detect DR in its early stages when symptoms are minimal, making early intervention harder.

- Current models may not fully leverage advanced feature extraction methods, limiting classification accuracy.
- High computational complexity hinders real-time application of DR detection in clinical settings.
- Retinal images vary in quality, contrast, and lighting, which affects model performance, especially for low-quality images.
- DR datasets often have more healthy samples than those with advanced DR, causing biased models that perform poorly on severe cases.
- Transfer learning is underutilized in DR research, which could enhance model performance with limited data.

Challenges:

- More healthy images than DR images that leads to model bias.
- Both deep learning and traditional models need a lot of processing power that makes it hard for real-time use.
- Combining DL and traditional ML models can be difficult and complex.
- Deep learning models can overfit small datasets, affecting generalization.
- Deep learning models lack transparency, making it hard for doctors to trust the results.
- Selecting the right features from both deep learning and traditional models is challenging.
- Ensuring models work quickly in clinical environments is tough due to their heavy computational demands.
- Making models scalable to large datasets from different sources can be difficult.
- It's complicated to train models that combine both deep learning and traditional machine learning techniques.

2.4 Summary

This thesis reviewed existing literature on diabetic retinopathy (DR) detection and examined the strengths and limitations of deep learning (DL), machine learning (ML) and hybrid methods. DL models demonstrated superior capabilities in feature extraction and classification accuracy, whereas ML methods relied on handcrafted features and traditional classifiers. Hybrid frameworks, which united DL and ML, leveraged the opposite advantages of both methods. However, despite their contributions, previous studies encountered challenges such as handling imbalanced datasets, detection of early-stage DR, variations in image quality, and adapting to real-world clinical complexities. These challenges underscore the need for more robust, efficient, and unified methods for DR detection and diagnosis.

Chapter 3
A Multimodal Approach for Dr Detection

CHAPTER 3
A MULTIMODAL APPROACH FOR DR DETECTION

3.1 Introduction

Diabetes mellitus is the underlying cause of diabetic retinopathy, a condition that affects the retina and is the leading cause of blindness worldwide. Early detection and treatment are crucial to slow down or prevent vision deterioration and loss of sight. To address this, researchers have proposed various artificial intelligence (AI) algorithms to identify and classify diabetic retinopathy from retinal fundus images. In this study, we present a method for the early detection and prediction of diabetic retinopathy using a Convolutional Neural Network (CNN). The deep CNN was trained and tested using a range of hyperparameters, including epoch size, batch size, and optimization techniques. Our dataset included examples of both normal and abnormal retinal images. The experimental results were evaluated using machine learning and deep learning approaches including Artificial Neural Networks (ANN), Support Vector Machines (SVM) and CNNs. Among these, the CNN achieved the highest accuracy and reaching 96.60% outperforming both SVM and other ANN models.

3.2 Proposed Methodology

Stacking many conventional convolutional layers can lead to the problem of vanishing gradients, which makes it difficult to optimize the network weights. Despite this, the traditional U-Net architecture has demonstrated high accuracy in segmentation tasks. To improve the training of deeper networks, the encoder's initial basic convolutional unit has been replaced with four residual blocks. To better capture both low-level and high-level features and give greater importance to the most relevant channels, the decoder has been enhanced with attention gate (AG) and squeeze-and-excitation (SE) blocks. These additions help compensate for the information loss caused by downsampling in the encoder.

Figure 3.1 illustrates the proposed CNN architecture along with the equipment used for acquiring fluorescence images, data processing, and training and testing the networks. This system is applied to detect oil leaks in transformers, as described below.

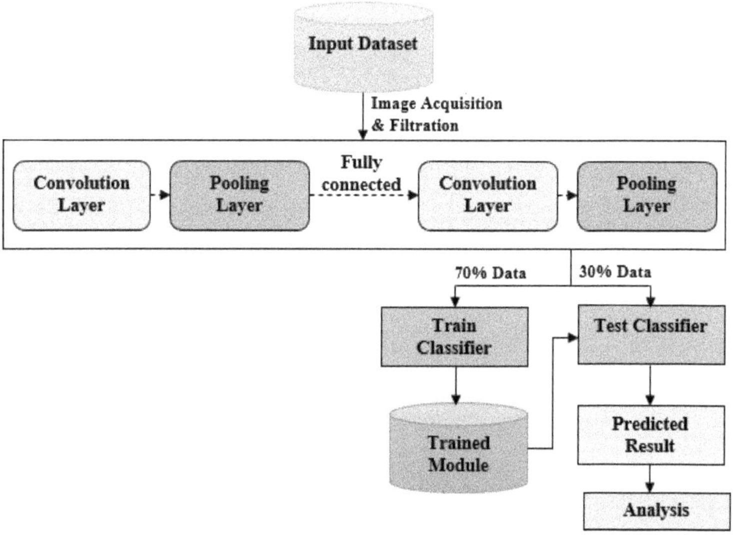

Figure 3.1: Proposed Framework

The dataset contains disorganized images, and there is a risk that it may become imbalanced over time. In the second phase, we applied essential preprocessing and normalization to the entire dataset to maximize accuracy for both training and testing. Preprocessing helps remove distortions for making subsequent processing more effective.

The preprocessing steps like cropping, color adjustment, smoothing and enhancement depend on image clarity with additional filtering applied as needed. For eye object detection and noise removal, YOLOv3 was used to highlight object boundaries and eliminate background interference. Image analysis focused on texture, color and shape with color assessed via moments and histograms, texture via uniformity, contrast, entropy, and variety and shape via area, roundness, concavity and irregularity.

Different features are important for different datasets; however, texture has been found to be the most crucial attribute for identifying plant diseases. Various techniques are employed to extract these features during the processing stage. Segmentation not only emphasizes key elements but also divides the image into distinct, meaningful regions. A useful feature of a well-segmented image is the number of histogram peaks, which helps accurately distinguish between healthy and diseased samples. Techniques such as thresholding, edge detection, color-based segmentation and position detection have all proven effective in plant disease detection. Color-based segmentation of spots, in particular, leverages the noticeable differences in color between the diseased area of a leaf and its healthy tissue.

3.2.1 Algorithm Design

Input Data: The process requires two datasets: a Training Dataset ($Train\_Data[]$) and Testing Dataset ($Test\_Data[]$).The key configuration settings for the model are required: "epoch size, batch size and the learning rate".

Output Goal: The final output is a class prediction for new data: "normal or abnormal".

Step 1: Initialize the Model

Set up the fundamental architecture and parameters for the neural network. This includes defining the size of the hidden layer and setting the initial values for the training process (batch size and epoch size).

Step 2: Prepare the Test Data Features

Read the Testing Dataset and convert it into a set of features.

$$test\_Features[tf] = \sum_{k=1}^{m} \left(Attribute.val\left[i,...,n\right] test\_data \right)$$

Step 3: Prepare the Training Data Features

Similarly, read the Training Dataset and convert it into a set of features.

$$train\_Features[tf] = \sum_{k=1}^{m} \left(Attribute.val\left[i,...,n\right] train\_data \right)$$

Step 4: Extract and Generate the Test Feature Map

From the normalized test information, extract an enhanced set of features to create a Test Feature Map.

$$Test_{FeatureMap[x,...n]} = Fset + \sum_{i=1}^{m} optimized\left((Fset)test\_Features[tf]\right)$$

Step 5: Extract and Generate the Train Feature Map

From the normalized training information, extract an enhanced set of features to create a Train Feature Map

$$Traint_{FeatureMap[x,...n]} = Fset + \sum_{i=1}^{m} optimized\left((Fset)train\_Features[tf]\right)$$

Steps 1 to 4 were repeated until the full number of epochs was completed. Each CNN iteration produced optimized features, which were stored in the feature maps. After all epochs were finished, the output layer (w) was executed.

Step 6: The CNN constructs the output layer for the final classification using three activation functions: "tanh, sigmoid and ReLU".

$$Layer\_Weight = Calc\_Weight\left(Test_{FeatureMap[x,...n]} \parallel \sum_{i=1}^{n} Traint_{FeatureMap[x,...,n]}\right)$$

Step 7: Validate the above $(Layer\_Weig\ \ t)$ using the defined optimal threshold.

$$if\left(Layer\_Weight >= Th\right)$$

Step 8: $Output_{List}.insert(trainF.class_{label}, Layer\_Weig\ \ t)$

Step 9: Return $Out_{List}.optimized.\max[0]$

To generate a similarity score between two input objects, both the Train_Feature and Test_Feature attributes are required as inputs for the test classifier. These attributes represent the training instance and the testing instance, respectively. The denominator used to evaluate the result at each epoch layer is denoted by T . The J^t feature of the testing instance is represented by $T[j]$, while the k^t feature of the training instance is represented by $T[k]$.

Using the feature selection method, specific characteristics are extracted from both the training and testing instances, which are then processed through the similarity measurement function described in Step 5. The densely optimized results obtained through the CNN correspond to the number of occurrences that meet the defined threshold.

3.3 Results and Discussion

This section describes the hyperparameter values used during the development and training of the proposed CNN model. These parameters guided the model's construction and learning process is given ion **Table 3.1**. The corresponding data is illustrated in the graph below:

Table 3.1: Hyperparameter Values of the Constructed CNN

Stage	Hyperparameter	Value
Initialization	Bias	0s
Training	Beta-1	0.9
	Beta-2	0.9
	Learning rate	0.001
	Weight	Gloro Uniform
	Epsilon	None
	Optimizer Amsgrad	False
	Decay	0.0
	Batch size	32
	Epoch size	10
	Steps-per-epoch	80

3.3.1 Experimental Findings Using CNN

The proposed system was trained using multiple datasets. After experimenting with various layer configurations and hyperparameter values, it was found that a five-layer CNN combined with an appropriate data split ratio and other optimized parameters, produced satisfactory results. The performance of the proposed mask CNN model was evaluated based on the number of layers and categorized accordingly. Detailed experimental results, along with additional features and performance metrics are presented in the following sections. The experiments were conducted using the 5-layer CNN model with a 70:30 training-to-testing split ratio.

In this section, the 5-layer CNN classifier is built using a 70:30 data split. **Table 3.2** presents the relationship between model accuracy, learning rate, training time and number of epochs based on this split. The best performance was achieved with a 50 epochs, learning rate of 0.001 and a training time of 500 seconds that resulting in a high accuracy of 96.60%.

Table 3.2: Performance of the Proposed Convolutional Neural Network: Accuracy and Training Time

Learning Rate	Epochs	Time to train (Sec)	Accuracy (%)
0.01	10	196	88.81
	20	239	90.97
	50	639	91.30
	100	1353	93.50
0.001	10	185	92.91
	20	236	93.28
	50	505	96.60
	100	1232	96.06
0.005	10	201	93.05
	20	245	93.18
	50	560	90.72
	100	1138	91.28

Figure 3.2 shows a bar graph depicting the relationship between learning rate and training duration. Based on this data split, three learning rate values were selected for evaluation: "0.001, 0.005, and 0.01".

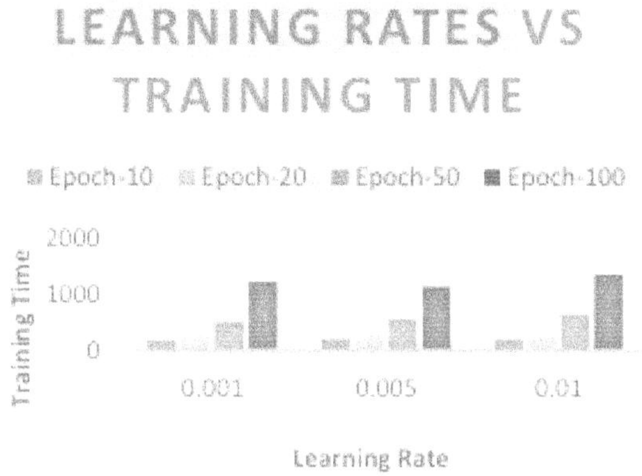

Figure 3.2: Training Time versus Learning Rate for the Proposed Convolutional Neural Network Model

Training time decreases as the learning rate increases. For a learning rate of 0.001 and 10 epochs, the training time is 185 seconds. **Figure 3.3** presents a bar graph showing the relationship between learning rate and accuracy. Based on this data split, four epoch values 10, 20, 50, and 100 were evaluated. The highest accuracy of 96.6% was achieved when the learning rate was 0.001.

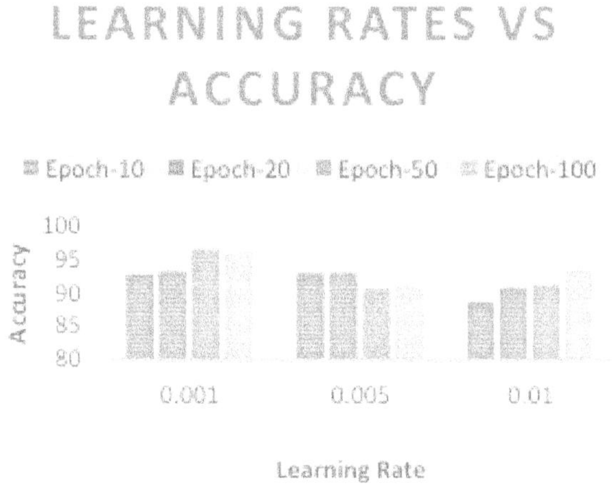

Figure 3.3: Effect of Learning Rate on Accuracy in the Proposed Convolutional Neural Network Model

3.4 Summary

This study proposes a multimodal approach combining machine learning and deep learning for detecting and predicting diabetic retinopathy. The framework particularly, CNNs effectively extracted retinal features, improving sensitivity, accuracy and specificity. The CNN achieved a detection accuracy of 96.60%, outperforming SVM and other neural network models. In summary, the multimodal integration of ML and DL methods offers a promising pathway for advancing DR detection and management, ultimately contributing to improved clinical outcomes and quality of life for patients. Future work should aim to refine these models further, incorporate diverse data sources and validate their performance in real-world clinical environments. Continued advancements in ML and DL combined with the growing availability of high-quality medical data are expected to drive ongoing progress in the accurate detection and prediction of diabetic retinopathy.

Chapter 4
Hybrid Deep Architecture

CHAPTER 4

HYBRID DEEP ARCHITECTURE

4.1 Introduction

Diabetic retinopathy (DR) detection, when relying on a single imaging modality like Optical Coherence Tomography (OCT) or fundus images, often falls brief in capturing the full range of structural and textural details required for accurate diagnosis. Fundus images offer surface-level information, while OCT captures cross-sectional details of retinal layers. A multimodal approach that integrates both OCT and fundus images offers a more comprehensive analysis to mitigate these drawbacks. This research offers a hybrid method combines these two imaging modalities to improve the segmentation as well as classification accuracy for DR detection.

The process starts with Gaussian filtering to preprocess the images, removing noise and smoothing both OCT and fundus images to enhance their quality. The denoised images are then segmented using an Improved ResUNet (ImResUNet) architecture, which utilized residual blocks and a self-attention mechanism to preserve contextual information across multiple scales. After segmentation, key features are extracted like deep and statistical features from OCT images and PHOG, Improved Shape Local Binary Pattern (ImSLBT) from fundus images. Particularly, the ImSLBT is effective at capturing strong local textures while remaining invariant to changes in illumination.

Then, the extracted features from modalities are fused using a Left-to-Right fusion strategy, which merges OCT and fundus data into a unified feature set. Subsequently, this fused feature set is passed into an Improved GoogLeNet model with Transfer Learning (ImGLN-TL) for diabetic retinopathy detection. The dual-network and the novel log-cosh focal Dice loss function enhance classification performance as well as convergence robustness. The outcome of the detection stage is inputted into a hybrid Bi-LSTM-SqueezeNet (Bi-LSTM-SN) model to predict the stage-wise progression of diabetic retinopathy,. In this model, Bi-LSTM captures temporal dependencies, while SqueezeNet reduces the feature dimensionality through Fire modules, providing the final prediction of DR progression.

4.2 Proposing an Advanced DL Model for DR Detection Using Multiple Modalities

A novel DL method that utilized multimodal imaging is presented in this research, which includes fundus photography and OCT, to enhance early detection and stage-by-stage progression forecasting of DR. The proposed method is outlined as below:

- **Data Collection and Preprocessing:** Initial phase includes obtaining OCT and fundus images, which are preprocessed via Gaussian filtering. This process effectively removes noise as well as improves the quality of the image, thus enhancing the consistency of following stages.
- **Segmentation:** Subsequently preprocessing, the image undergoes segmentation through an improved ResUNet (ImResUNet) model. This model includes residual blocks and a self-attention mechanism, which allows for more accurate and contextual segmentation of retinal structures in both OCT image and fundus image.
- **Feature Extraction:** During the feature extraction stage, deep features and statistical features are derived from the OCT images, which combines PHOG descriptors and an ImSLBT are extracted from the fundus images. Especially, the ImSLBT effective for capturing detailed texture variations and is improves to changes in lighting conditions.
- **Feature Fusion:** From both modalities, the extracted features are integrated via a Left-to-Right fusion approach. This technique efficiently combines complementary features from the OCT and fundus images, which created a unified, improved representation for additional analysis.
- **Classification:** An enhanced GoogLeNet model with Transfer Learning (ImGLN-TL) is employed for classification. It incorporates a dual-network configuration along with a log-cosh focal Dice loss function, which enhances model convergence, addressing class imbalance and strengthening a more robust classification process.

- **Stage-wise DR Prediction:** The output from the classification phase is inputted into a hybrid Bi-LSTM-SqueezeNet model to forecast the stage-by-stage progression of Diabetic Retinopathy. The Bi-LSTM captures temporal dependencies, while SqueezeNet reduces spatial features. The joint output of these two networks provides an accurate prediction of DR progression over time. **Figure 4.1** establishes the overall process of the DR forecasting system.

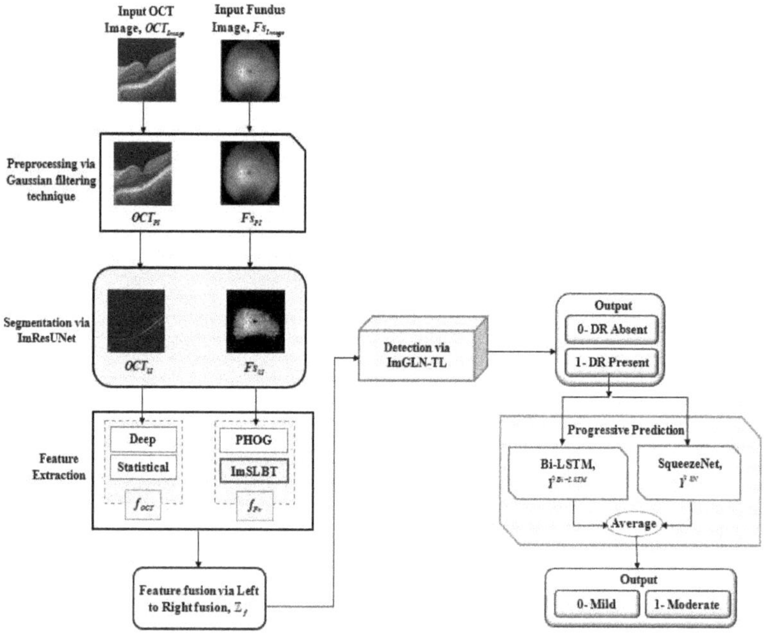

Figure 4.1: Proposed Multimodal DL Framework for DR detection and progression prediction.

4.2.1 Applying Gaussian Filtering for Preprocessing

In the proposed framework, the input images, including Optical Coherence Tomography (OCT) images, referred to as OCT Image, OCT_{Image} and fundus images, FS_{Image} , undergoes a preprocessing step to clean and reduce noise before segmentation and feature extraction. Gaussian filtering [91] is utilized as the primary preprocessing method because it effectively removes well-distributed noise while preserving important structural details in medical images. The result of this preprocessing step is the smoothed images, signified as OCT_{PI} and Ps_{PI}.

Gaussian filtering is a linear, low-pass filter where each pixel's new value is calculated as a weighted sum of its neighboring pixels, with the weights evaluated by a two-dimensional Gaussian function. The Gaussian filter kernel $G_f\ (x'\ ,\ y'\ )$ is computed using Eq. (4.1), wherein, σ' implies the Gaussian kernel's standard deviation, which controls the level of smoothing and the constant normalizes the total weight to equal one. This filtering technique smooths both OCT and fundus images by suppressing high-frequency noise, thus enhancing the consistency and effectiveness of following segmentation processes.

$$G_f(x', y') = \frac{1}{-} e^{\frac{(x'^2 + y'^2)}{2\sigma'^2}} \tag{4.1}$$

4.2.2 Advancements in Segmentation with ImResUNet through Self-Attention Mechanism

After preprocessing, the denoised OCT images OCT_{PI} and fundus images Fs_{PI} undergo a segmentation process to identify key retinal structures. Accurate segmentation is crucial for isolating areas that are characteristic of DR. An improved ResUNet model (ImResUNet) is proposed to achieve this. It is designed to improve the retention of contextual and hierarchical information in medical images, ensuring more precise segmentation. The ImResUNet improves the ability to capture and preserve critical details that are essential for identifying DR-related features in both OCT and fundus images.

Conventional ResUNet

The conventional ResU-Net structure [92] builds upon the original U-Net by including residual blocks into both the encoder and decoder paths. The model employs convolutions, max-pooling and upsampling methods to handle 3D input data. Individually residual block enables the network to train identity mappings, which helps mitigate vanishing gradient problems as well as supports the training of deeper networks. ResU-Net typically outperforms the basic U-Net model. for biomedical segmentation tasks. In training, a balanced cross-entropy loss function is commonly employed to mitigate class imbalance problems.

While the ResU-Net model includes residual connections to aid in training deep networks, it struggles to preserve long-term related associations and deeper classified semantics, which is particularly in multimodal medical images like fundus image and OCT image. This drawback prevents the model from effectively learning intricate spatial patterns as well as interlayer dependencies. Consequently, the segmented outputs may lose fine boundary details or perform poorly in complex pathological zones, which makes them less reliable for diabetic retinopathy performance.

Improved ResU-Net Architecture (ImResUNet)

An improved ResU-Net (ImResUNet) model is introduced to address these limitations, which incorporating an enhanced self-attention mechanism (ImSAM) in each encoder and decoder block. The encoder starts by passing the preprocessed images through a convolutional layer and a residual block to learn low-level features. These are then processed by the improved self-attention mechanism (ImSAM), which finds spatial relationships and highlights key features. The resultant feature is passed through a convolution layer, which is followed by an activation function (tanh).

Subsequent encoder stages follow a similar pattern: max-pooling, convolution, residual block, and ImSAM. The decoder path mirrors this architecture, with upsampling, convolution, residual block and ImSAM, including corresponding skip connections from the encoder blocks to secure spatial information. The final output is produced through a Transposed Convolution (TransConv), which results in the segmented images OCT_{SI} and Fs_{SI}. The structure of the ImResUNet model is depicting in **Figure 4.2**.

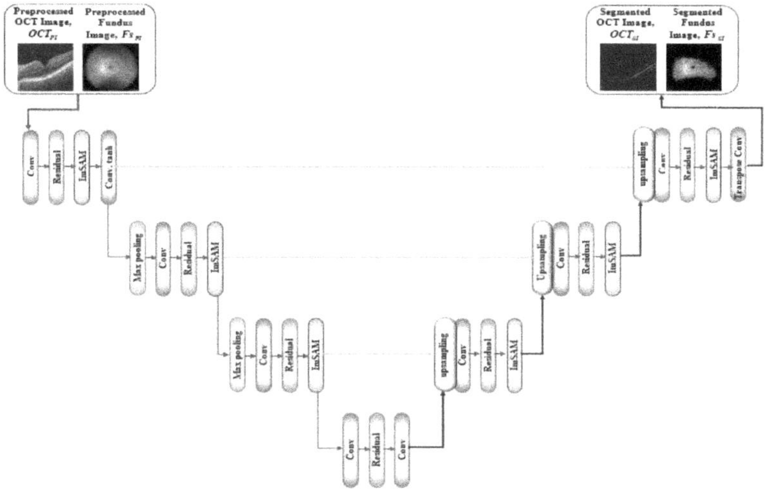

Figure 4.2: Architecture of P-ResU-Net

Proposed ImSAM

The improved self-attention mechanism (ImSAM) is integrated into every encoder and decoder block of the ImResUNet structure to enhances the ability of the model to train spatial relationships and focus on the most informative areas in OCT and fundus images. Given an input feature sequence $_t = [\ {}^{\wedge}_1, \ldots, {}^{\wedge}_t\ ]$, the attention module [93] computes a set of attention weights, which reflect the relative importance of each feature in contributing to the target output.

(a) Improved Score Alignment

Eq. (4.2) defines the standard score function, wherein, $\aleph_{att}$ signifies the trainable weight matrix and ℓ_{att} means the bias vector. This feature allows the model to capture important information about the input features but may be less sensitive to fine-grained variations, especially in challenging medical image data.

$$sa_t = \tanh(\ _t \cdot \aleph_{att} + \ell_{att}) \tag{4.2}$$

A non-linear improved scoring function is introduced to address this issue, which is based on a Hard Hyperbolic Softmax (HHSM) activation and additional regularization terms. Eq. (4.3) defines the improved scoring function, where the

HHSM activation introduces non-linearity to prevent attention saturation, which described in Eq. (4.4).

$$sa_{t,new} = \left\{ \frac{HHSM\left({}_{t} \cdot \aleph_{att} + \left[\frac{e^{t} - e^{-t}}{e^{t} + e^{-t}} \right] * \ell_{att} \right)}{{}_{t} * \log\left(1 + e^{t}\right)} \right\} \quad (4.3)$$

$$HHSM = \begin{cases} -1 & if \quad {}_{t} < -1 \\ {}_{t} & {}_{t} \leq 1 \\ 1 & {}_{t} > 1 \end{cases} \quad (4.4)$$

(b) *Improved attention weight*

Once the scores $sa_{t,new}$ are obtained, a Softmax function is processed to calculate the attention weights $a\varpi$, as given in Eq. (4.5). An improved weight computation strategy is employed in the ImSAM layer, which is computed according to Eq. (4.6). wherein, $\theta = arccos\,(1/3)$ is a constant used for trigonometric modulation, allowing for the adjustment of attention intensity across different feature dimensions. This method allows the model to refine weights more effectively, which based on the local complexity of the features.

$$a\varpi_{t} = softmax(sa_{t}) \quad (4.5)$$

$$a\varpi_{t,new} = \left\{ \frac{HHSM\left(sa_{t,new} + \left(1 - \ln\left(1 + e^{(sa_{t,new} + {}_{t})}\right)\right)\right)}{\frac{1}{2} \cdot \cos\theta \, \square_{t} \cdot \aleph_{att}} \right\} \quad (4.6)$$

(c) *Improved context vector*

The attention mechanism's final step is the creation of the context vector (i.e., attention output), which implies a input features weighted sum based on their importance scores. Traditionally, this is calculated according to Eq. (4.7). An additional mean-based term is introduced in ImSAM, to enhance feature diversity and robustness, which is described in Eq. (4.8). Here, μ implies the statistical mean-based regularize, which is computed in Eq. (4.9).

$$av_t = \sum_{i=1}^{T} a\varpi_t \quad _t \tag{4.7}$$

$$av_{t,new} = \sum_{i=1}^{T} a\varpi_{t,new} \quad _t + \mu(\quad _t) \tag{4.8}$$

$$\mu = \left[\frac{\sum_{i=T}^{T} (\quad _t)^2}{\sum_{i=1} (\quad _t)} \right] \tag{4.9}$$

This additional term allows the attention output to be inclined by local activation levels as well as global statistical characteristics, allowing the network to capture subtle variations and enhance interpretability.

As a result, the ImResUNet model integrates ImSAM and residual connections to more effectively capture crucial features during segmentation. This advances its capability to preserve contextual information and generalize across different types of images. The multi-level feature refinement ensures stable and accurate segmentation for both OCT and fundus images.

4.2.3 Extraction of Multimodal Features from OCT and Fundus Images

Once OCT and fundus images segmented, the subsequent crucial step is to extract their features. Here, the goal is to attain significant and discriminative features from the segmented regions that will support robust classification. For the OCT segmented image, OCT_{SI} features such as deep learning-based features such as VGG-16 and ResNet and statistical features are extracted. For the fundus segmented image, Fs_{SI} features like PHOG and ImSLBT are used. The extracted features from OCT images represented as $F_{\propto T}$ and the extracted features from fundus images is denotes as f_{Fs}.

4.2.3.1 VGG-16 and ResNet Feature Extraction from OCT images

Deep feature extractor VGG-16 [94] is used its proven effectiveness in visual pattern recognition tasks. In this architecture, the early convolutional layers, edges and textures (low-level features) are capture, while the deeper layers recognize more complex patterns associated with pathological and structural differences. The last fully connected layers' outcome generates a high-dimensional depiction of the OCT_{SI} , capturing crucial features relevant to disease classification. VGG-16 is composed of thirteen convolutional layers and three fully connected layers, enabling it to capture intricate feature hierarchies. Although it is computationally demanding, its ability to learn sophisticated feature distributions makes it a valuable component in the flow.

Further enhances deep feature extraction, ResNet (Residual Network) [95] by addressing the degradation problem commonly encountered in very DNNs. The short links and identity mappings in ResNet facilitate smoother gradient flow through the network, allowing deeper models to be trained without a loss in performance. Each ResNet module contains two 3x3 convolutional layers with ReLU activations, BN and an element-wise addition of the input. This design significantly boosts the model's ability to extract features, particularly fine details in OCT images, OCT_{SI} including structures and pathologies.

4.2.3.2 Statistical Features from OCT Images

In addition to deep features, statistical features [96] are extracted to capture the texture and intensity characteristics of segmented OCT image, OCT_{SI} . These features aid in differentiating between healthy and pathological regions by taking the underlying variations in pixel intensity patterns.

Mean: Its intensity is a fundamental statistical measure representing the average brightness level within the segmented OCT area. Alterations in tissue density, particularly in DR-affected retinal images, which can result in average intensity noticeable changes.

Median: Its intensity value serves as a more robust measure of central tendency. Unlike the mean, the median is less influenced by extreme pixel values or noise. This is particularly useful in OCT images, where isolated bright or dark regions may distort the mean intensity, but have little impact on the median.

Standard deviation: It is used to assess the intensity variation in the segmented OCT image. A higher standard deviation indicates more complex texture, making it an important feature for identifying pathological regions It measures the deviation of pixel intensities from the mean, providing an estimate of tissue heterogeneity.

Minimum and Maximum: Their intensity values capture the grayscale range of variation within the segmented OCT image. The minimum value highlights the darkest areas, which may correspond to hyper-reflective regions, while the maximum intensity value identifies the brightest features, typically associated with hyper-reflective spots.

Together, these statistical features, —mean, median, standard deviation, minimum, and maximum‖, which offers a compact nonetheless informative summary of the segmented retinal area. When combined with deep features and other descriptors, they enhance the robustness and interpretability of the feature set used for classifying and diagnosing DR.

4.2.3.3 PHOG Extraction from Fundus Images

To capture shape and texture information across different spatial scales, the Pyramid Histogram of Oriented Gradients (PHOG) [97] is used for the segmented fundus images Fs_{SI} . The PHOG descriptor splits the image into spatial grids at multiple pyramid levels, and for each grid cell, it computes the HOG using the Sobel operator. The gradient magnitude $\vec{g}$ and direction θ are calculated according to Eq. (4.10).

$$\vec{g} = \sqrt{\vec{g}_a^{\,2} + \vec{g}_b^{\,2}} \tag{4.10}$$

$$\theta = arct\left(\frac{\vec{g}_a}{\vec{g}_b}\right) \tag{4.11}$$

In this equation, $\vec{g}_a$ represent the gradients along the x axes and $\vec{g}_b$ represent the gradients along the y axes. Then, compute the orientation histograms for each pyramid level and aggregated. These histograms from all levels are then concatenated to form the PHOG descriptor. This method retains both spatial and edge orientation details, which are essential in fundus images for accurately describing the anatomical structures.

4.2.3.4 Improved SLBT (ImSLBT) for Fundus Image Texture

In the feature extraction of Fs_{SI} , the ImSLBT is applied to capture various texture-based features, as illustrated in **Figure 4.3**. The SLBT [98] builds upon the traditional Local Binary Pattern (LBP) technique, enhancing its ability to preserve local spatial details and better distinguish subtle structural variations in fundus images. Additionally, LBP is effective at capturing micro textures, which play a critical role in analyzing pathological regions in medical images.

The conventional LBP technique functions by comparing the intensity of a central pixel with its eight neighboring pixels within a 3x3 window. Each surrounding pixel $\wp_c$ is individually assessed against the center pixel $\wp_l$ and a binary value is assigned based on the comparison outcome. These binary digits are then weighted according to their positions and summed to produce a single decimal number, forming the LBP code, as defined in Eq. (4.12). The corresponding function $\xi(k)$ is defined in Eq. (4.13). While this method effectively generates a local binary representation for each image patch, it lacks sensitivity to subtle intensity variations and detailed spatial structures, which can limit its descriptive power in certain situations.

$$LBP(\hat{x}_c, \hat{y}_c) = \sum_{l=0} \xi(\wp_l - \wp_c) 2^l \tag{12}$$

$$\xi(k) = \begin{cases} 1, & k \geq 0 \\ 0, & k < 0 \end{cases} \tag{13}$$

Though conventional LBP [99] is known for its simplicity and computational efficiency, it fails to capture critical intensity relationships and statistical variations within image patches. This limitation is particularly problematic in medical imaging, where minor texture differences often carry significant diagnostic value. To address this issue, an ImSLBT method is proposed. This approach incorporates both the mean and variance of the neighborhood, along with a uniformity measure, to better preserve spatial and statistical texture patterns. The ImSLBT enhances the standard LBP by integrating statistical parameters, as defined in Eq. (4.14), where v signifies the neighborhood variance, which is evaluated using Eq. (4.15), μ implies the mean using Eq. (4.16) and W_k implies the average neighbor pixel value. The function κ is computed using Eq. (4.17). Moreover, CHM and IQM refer to the Contra Harmonic Mean and Interquartile Mean, respectively. The uniform local binary pattern operator, denoted as $U(LBP(\hat{x}_c, \hat{y}_c))$ is computed according to Eq. (4.18). By incorporating these statistical features, the SLBT descriptor becomes more responsive to subtle texture variations, which are often indicative of pathological changes in fundus images.

$$LBP(\hat{x}_c, \hat{y}_c)_{new} = \begin{cases} \sum_{l=0}^{l-1} \left(\xi(\wp_l - \wp_c)\right) \cdot (\nu + \kappa), & \text{if } \cup\left(LBP(\hat{x}_c, \hat{y}_c)\right) \le 2 \\ (l+1) \cdot (\nu + \kappa), & \text{otherwise} \end{cases} \tag{4.14}$$

$$\nu = \left[\frac{1}{l} \sum_{l=0}^{l-1} (\wp_l - \mu)^2\right] \tag{4.15}$$

$$\mu = \frac{1}{l} \sum_{l=0}^{l-1} W_k \frac{(\wp_l - \wp_c)^2}{(\wp_l + \wp_c)} \tag{4.16}$$

$$\kappa = \begin{cases} 1, & \text{if } CHM \ge \wp_l \text{ and } IQM \le \wp_c \\ 0, & \text{else if } IQM \ge \wp_l \text{ and } IQM > \wp_c \\ 1, & \text{else if } IQM < \wp_l \text{ and } \wp_l \le \wp_c \\ 0, & \text{otherwise} \end{cases} \tag{4.17}$$

$$\cup\left(LBP(\hat{x}_c, \hat{y}_c)\right) = \left|\xi(\wp_{l-1} - \wp_c) - \xi(\wp_0 - \wp_c)\right| + \sum_{l=0}^{l} \left|\xi\left((\wp_l * \kappa) - (\wp_c * \nu)\right) - \xi\left((\wp_{l+1} * (\kappa + \nu)) - \wp_c\right)\right| \tag{4.18}$$

Therefore, ImSLBT establishes greater robustness to minor intensity fluctuations and illumination variations, which are commonly encountered in real-world medical imaging scenarios. Furthermore, by preserving essential spatial structures and incorporating sensitivity to texture variability, it significantly enhances the model's ability to distinguish between visually similar textures that may arise from different pathological conditions.

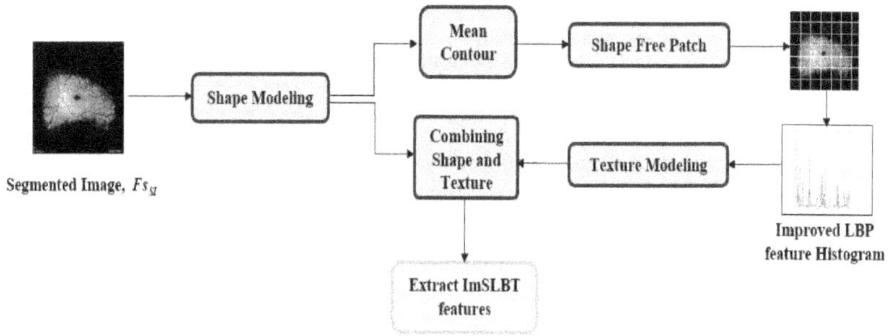

Figure 4.3: Diagrammatic representation of ImSLBT

Lastly, the features extracted from the OCT images like deep features from models like VGG-16 and ResNet, as well as statistical measures—are represented as $f_{\propto T}$. Similarly, features derived from fundus images, such as PHOG and ImSLBT descriptors, are denoted as f_{Fs} . These feature vectors are subsequently passed through the fusion and classification stages, enabling accurate disease detection based on integrated multimodal information.

4.2.4 Multimodal feature fusion via Left to Right fusion strategy

During the feature fusion stage is designed to effectively integrate the features extracted from $f_{\propto T}$ and f_{Fs} to capitalize on the complementary strengths of both modalities. While OCT images provide detailed cross-sectional structural information, fundus images contribute surface-level texture characteristics. To achieve an optimal balance between these two types of data, a smooth fusion strategy known as Left-to-Right Fusion [100] is employed. This method facilitates the seamless merging of feature sets, enhancing the overall representation. The fusion process involves the following sequential steps.

Step (i): Begin by extracting relevant features from the OCT images, $f_{\propto T}$

Step (ii): Next, extract features from the fundus images, f_{Fs}

Step (iii): Identify and store the number of columns in the extracted feature matrices.

Step (iv): Construct a linearly spaced vector ranging from 0 to 1, with a length equal to the column size, C

Step (5): Execute the fusion by applying an element-wise multiplication of the feature sets using Eq. (4.19).

$$f = \left(f_{OCT} \otimes C\right) + \left(f_{Fs} \otimes (1 - C)\right) \tag{4.19}$$

Lastly, the fused feature vector f is fed into the improved GoogLeNet (ImGLN-TL) model enhanced with transfer learning for the purpose of diabetic retinopathy detection.

4.2.5 Multimodal DR Detection via ImGLN-TL

The detection phase of the proposed work employs an Improved GoogLeNet model integrated with transfer learning (ImGLN-TL) to regulate the presence or absence of DR based on the fused features f, which are derived from both OCT and fundus images. As illustrated in **Figure 4.4**, the DR detection process follows a two-stage network architecture, where two Improved GoogLeNet (ImGLN) models are employed sequentially. In the first stage, the initial ImGLN is trained via the combined multimodal features. The output weights from this model are then passed as input to a second ImGLN network. This second model, trained on the same feature space, produces the final binary classification output: —0‖ signifying the —absence of DR‖ and —1‖ signifying its —presence of DR‖.

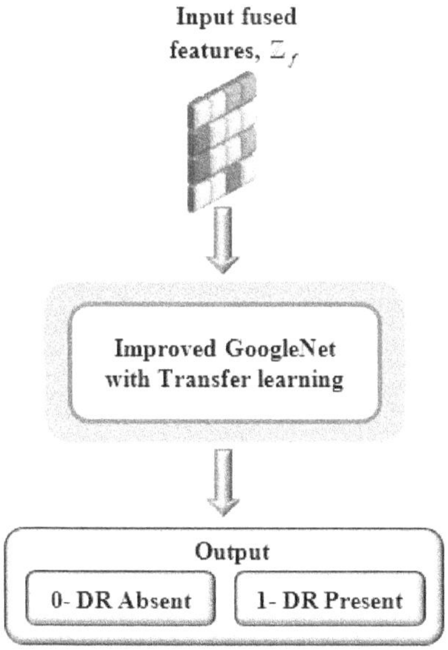

Figure 4.4: Overall process of Multimodal DR Detection process

The approach relies on transfer learning, where the higher-level network is firstly trained on a large source dataset and subsequently fine-tuned on a smaller, related target dataset. This process allows the model to leverage generalized low-level features such as edges and textures, learned from the source task, while focusing on DR-specific patterns during fine-tuning. Transfer learning not only accelerates the convergence rate but also helps prevent overfitting, which makes it particularly well-suited for medical imaging datasets. This DR detection is depicting in **Figure 4.5**.

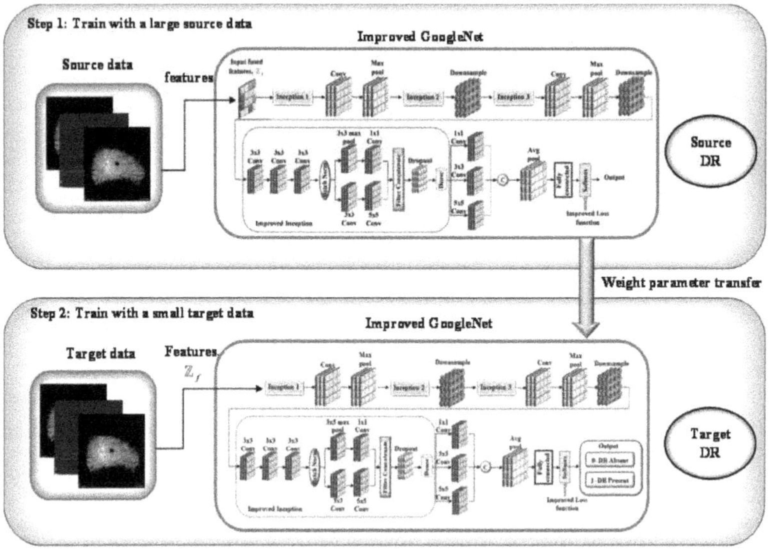

Figure 4.5: Process of *ImGLN-TL* model

Traditional GLN architecture

Traditional GLN [101] is a DCNN composed of nine inception layers that progressively learn hierarchical feature representations. The framework begins with a large 7x7 convolutional layer, which is followed by alternating max-pooling and convolutional layers. These layers are succeeded by inception modules, which apply multiple filters of varying sizes such as 1x1, 3x3, 5x5 in parallel and concatenate their outputs to capture multi-scale features effectively. A local loss is computed after every three inception layers to maintain training efficiency. The network concludes with average pooling and a fully connected layer that transforms the extracted features for classification using a softmax output. However, since this study focuses on binary classification, the final softmax layer is replaced with a specialized function tailored for binary outputs.

Improved GoogLeNet model

Although conventional GoogLeNet performs well, it faces challenges such as vanishing or exploding gradients and an increased risk of overfitting due to its deep layers and complex module stacking. To mitigate these issues, the current study proposes an Improved GoogLeNet (ImGLN) architecture designed for enhanced stability, efficiency, and multi-scale feature extraction, as illustrated in **Figure 4.6**. The fused features f are first processed through the initial inception block, followed by a convolutional layer and max-pooling. The resulting output then passes sequentially through a second inception block, a downsample layer, and subsequently a third inception block along with additional convolutional as well as pooling layers. After that, the features are fed into a newly designed Improved Inception block for deeper abstraction.

In the Improved Inception block, the input first passes through three successive 3x3 convolutional layers, BN to stabilize the learning process. Next, the data flows into two parallel streams: the first applies a 3x3 max-pooling layer a 1x1 convolution, while the second performs a 3x3 convolution trailed by a 5x5 convolution. The outputs from these two branches, along with the original input, are then concatenated using a filter concatenation layer to integrate multi-scale features. This combined feature map is passed through a dropout layer to reduce overfitting and then fed into a dense layer for further feature learning. Subsequently, the output is processed through three convolutional layers with kernel sizes of 1x1, 3x3, and 5x5 and their results are concatenated and passed to an average pooling layer that was followed by another fully connected layer. Finally, the output is directed into a softmax layer to perform binary classification.

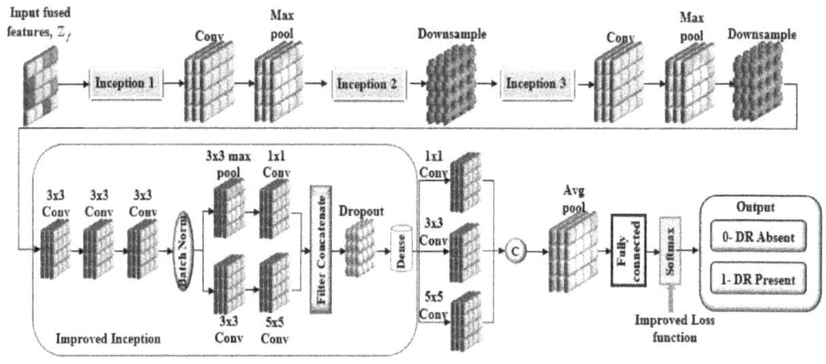

Figure 4.6: Process of ImGLN model

Improved Loss function

The ImGLN employs a Log-cosh Focal Dice Loss function to further improve convergence and robustness. While the traditional Dice Loss [102], defined in Eq. (4.20), measures the similarity between predicted labels actual labels, it is prone to issues such as exploding gradients and over fitting. The proposed Log-cosh Focal Dice Loss addresses these challenges by regularizing the loss landscape and stabilizing training, as described in Eq. (4.21). Here L_{FDL} signifies the focal dice loss function, calculated using Eq. (4.22), where α means trainable parameter constrained within the range [0, 1].

$$Dice\ Loss\left(\square,\hat{\square}\right)=\left[1-\frac{2\square\hat{\square}+1}{\square+\hat{\square}+1}\right] \tag{4.20}$$

$$Loss_{LC-DL}=\left[\log\left(\cosh\left(L_{FDL}\right)\right)\right] \tag{4.21}$$

$$L_{FDL}=\left[-\alpha\left(1-\frac{2\square\hat{\square}+1}{\square+\hat{\square}+1}\right)^{\gamma}\log\left(\hat{\square}+1\right)\right],\quad \gamma>0 \tag{4.22}$$

The inception modules' parallel convolutions with multiple kernel sizes effectively capture features at different scales while decreasing the number of parameters. This design minimizes the risk of overfitting and allows for deeper network architectures without suffering from vanishing gradients. Additionally, dimensionality reduction is incorporated within the inception blocks, which further improves gradient flow and training efficiency. The improved loss function also contributes to increased classification accuracy.

4.2.6 Progressive Prediction of DR using Bi-LSTM-SqueezeNet

To accurately predict the progression of DR), a hybrid deep learning model combining Bi-Directional Long Short-Term Memory (Bi-LSTM) and SqueezeNet (SN) is proposed. This model is activated only when the detection phase outputs —1‖ indicating the —presence of DR‖. By leveraging the sequential characteristics of disease progression, this phase enhances the system's ability to identify the stage-wise development of DR, as depicting in **Figure 4.7**.

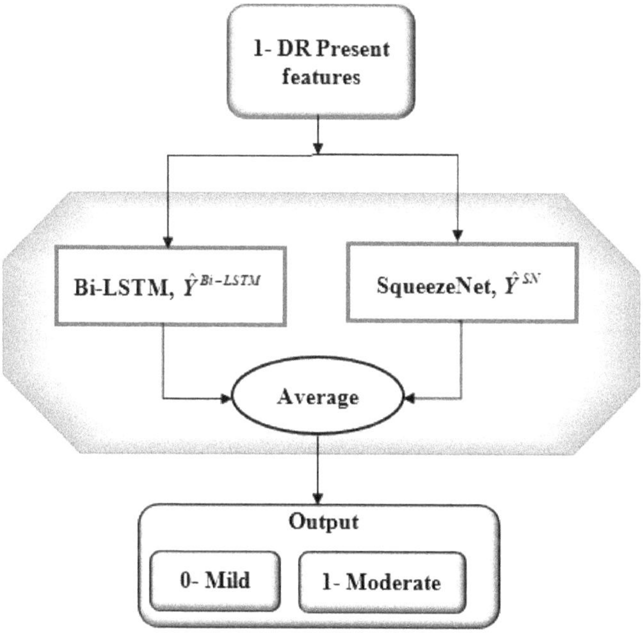

Figure 4.7: Diagrammatic representation of Progressive Prediction of DR

4.2.6.1 Bi-LSTM

The combined feature vectors indicating the presence of DR are fed into a Bi-LSTM network [103] to capture the temporal dependencies in the progression of DR. Unlike standard LSTM, sequences processes in a single forward direction and may overlook future context, Bi-LSTM employs two parallel LSTM layers that process the sequence both forward and backward. This architecture allows the model to effectively incorporate information from both past and future time steps at each moment. At each time step $t^\wedge$the forward hidden state $\hbar^{\rightarrow}{}_t$ is computed as described in Eq. (4.23), while the backward hidden state ${}^{\rightarrow}\hbar_t$ is calculated according to Eq. (4.24), where χ represents the input presence of DR. The final hidden representation at time $t^\wedge$ is obtained by concatenating these two states, as shown in Eq. (4.25).

$$\overrightarrow{}_t = LSTM\left(\chi_t, \overrightarrow{}_{t-1}\right) \tag{4.23}$$

$$\overrightarrow{}_t = LSTM\left(\chi_t, \overrightarrow{}_{t+1}\right) \tag{4.24}$$

$$_t = \left[\overrightarrow{}_t, \overrightarrow{}_t\right] \tag{4.25}$$

This encoding allows the Bi-LSTM model to more precisely recognize progression patterns of DR-related features, which is labelled as $\hat{Y}^{Bi-LSTM}$.

4.2.6.2 SqueezeNet for Progressive Prediction

SqueezeNet (SN) [104] complements it by efficiently extracting spatial features. SqueezeNet is a lightweight convolutional neural network consisting of an initial convolutional layer, followed by eight consecutive —Fire‖ modules, and a final convolutional layer. Each Fire module includes a —squeeze‖ layer with 1x1 filters and an —expand‖ layer that combines both 1x1 and 3x3 filters, significantly reducing the number of parameters while maintaining accuracy. The input to SqueezeNet, derived from the same merged feature vector used by the Bi-LSTM, passes through the Fire modules and pooling layers. After the ninth Fire module, the feature map undergoes dropout, a final convolutional layer, global average pooling, and a fully connected layer with softmax activation to predict the severity stage of DR, denoted as $\hat{Y}^{SN}$.

4.2.6.3 Fusion of Predictions for Final Output

The outputs from the Bi-LSTM $\hat{Y}^{Bi-LSTM}$ and SqueezeNet $\hat{Y}^{SN}$ branches are averaged to produce the final progression prediction. This dual-pathway design ensures that temporal and spatial features are both effectively utilized. The final classification is binary: —0‖ indicates mild progression, and —1‖ indicates moderate progression of diabetic retinopathy. This hybrid approach enhances robustness and reliability, especially in longitudinal assessments of the disease.

4.3 Results and Discussion

4.3.1 Simulation Procedure

The Early Detection and Progressive Prediction of Diabetic Retinopathy using Multimodal Imaging Techniques was simulated using —PYTHON 3.7‖. The processor employed was —Intel(R) Core(TM) i5-1035G1 CPU @ 1.00GHz 1.19 GHz and the Installed RAM size was 20.0 GB‖. Further, the dataset was collected manually.

4.3.2 Description of Dataset

In this research, the original dataset involved 372 samples. Subsequent data augmentation, the total amount of samples increased to 2,520. The dataset contains two distinct classes such as —No DR (Label 0)‖ and —DR (Label 1)‖. **Table 4.1** shows the data distribution between these classes for both the detection as well as classification stages, before and after augmentation.

Table 4.1: Data Distribution for Detection and Classification Stages

Classes			**NO DR**	**DR**
Detection Stage	Before Augmentation	Fundus	153	33
		OCT	153	33
	After Augmentation	Fundus	612	648
		OCT	612	648
Classification Stage	Before Augmentation	Fundus	27	6
		OCT	27	6
	After Augmentation	Fundus	324	324
		OCT	324	324

Subject	Ophthalmology.
Specific subject area	Diabetic Retinopathy
Data format	Raw Images, Excel file
Type of data	1. Fundus images with dimensions 3680 × 3288, 96 dpi, and jpeg 2. OCTA (8 × 8 mm) images with dimensions 1596 × 990, 96 dpi and jpeg 3. Annotations of the classifications are provided in an EXCEL file (.xlsx).
Data collection	This dataset contains OCTA and Fundus images. Nonmydriatic fundus images were acquired using a confocal SLO widefield fundus imaging Eidon machine and Nonmydriatic OCTA images were acquired using the Optovue Avanti Edition machine. OCTA and Fundus images are classified into three categories NO DR signs, Mild DR, and Moderate DR.
Data source location	The dataset of 222 images was acquired at the Natasha Eye Care and Research Centre, Shiv Sai Lane, Pimple Saudagar Pune 411017.
Data	Repository name: Multimodal OCTA and Fundus Image dataset for detection of
accessibility	Diabetic Retinopathy (Version-1) Data identification number: https://doi.org/10.5281/zenodo.8375220 Direct URL to data: https://zenodo.org/record/8375220 Data is under a data usage agreement. Instructions for accessing these data: Access will be given on prior permission specifying the use of the dataset and with proper citation and DOI

1. Value of the Data

The multimodal dataset serves as a valuable resource for both the medical scientific community and informatics researchers. It plays a crucial role in several aspects:

- This multimodal data set is particularly helpful for training and conducting research by novice experts who are interested in the examination of DR at the early stage.
- As this is a multimodal dataset with Fundus and OCTA images, by comparing this with normal images, the data set can be used to study retinal anatomy and its physiological variations within diabetic and nondiabetic

patients.

- Encouraging the creation of mathematical frameworks for automated medical diagnosis, particularly for the use of AI tools for detecting diabetic retinopathy (DR) early.
- Supporting the training of future physicians in identifying and analyzing various stages of DR using fundus and OCTA images.

2.

3. Data Description

Retinal or fundus images play a crucial role in the identification of various eye-related disorders. These images capture essential structures within the eye, including blood vessels, the optic disc, and the macula. The information derived from these structures in retinal images is instrumental in diagnosing and treating a range of retinal conditions [3], [4], [5].

The Early Treatment Diabetic Retinopathy Study (ETDRS) classifies diabetic retinopathy into two main categories: Non-Proliferative Diabetic Retinopathy (NPDR) and Proliferative Diabetic Retinopathy (PDR). NPDR represents the early stage of the disease and further divides into mild, moderate, severe, and very severe. On the other hand, PDR is a more advanced form and is categorized into early and advanced stages. Medical experts have categorized the dataset into three distinct groups based on the pathological conditions associated with diabetic retinopathy.

Consequently, the dataset is organized into three disease categories, including No DR signs, Mild (or early) NPDR, and Moderate NPDR For detailed information on the criteria used for classifying fundus images.

The Early Treatment Diabetic Retinopathy Study (ETDRS) classifies diabetic retinopathy into two main categories: Non-Proliferative Diabetic Retinopathy (NPDR) and Proliferative Diabetic Retinopathy (PDR). NPDR represents the early stage of the disease and further divides into mild, moderate, severe, and very severe. On the other hand, PDR is a more advanced form and is categorized into early and advanced stages. Medical experts have categorized the dataset into three distinct groups based on the pathological conditions associated with diabetic retinopathy. Consequently, the dataset is organized into three disease categories, including No DR signs, Mild (or early) NPDR, and Moderate NPDR For detailed information on the criteria used for classifying fundus images, please refer to [5]. The new dataset comprises 222 fundus and OCTA images of 76 persons where some patients have diabetes, and some patients don't have diabetes with corresponding labels and classification status available in the "Annotations of the classifications.xlsx" file.

Table 4.2: Illustration of a sample representation of diabetic retinopathy (DR) labels contained within the XLSX file.

Person	Image number	Image format	Classification Status
1	L1.1	JPEG	NO DR
	L1.2	JPEG	NO DR
4	L4.1	JPEG	MILD DR
	L4.2	JPEG	MILD DR
	R4.3	JPEG	MILD DR
	R4.4	JPEG	MILD DR
6	R6.1	JPEG	MODERATE DR
	R6.2	JPEG	MODERATE DR
53	L53.1	JPEG	MODERATE DR
Person	**Image number**	**Image format**	**Classification Status**
	L53.2	JPEG	MODERATE DR
	R53.3	JPEG	MILD DR
	R53.4	JPEG	MILD DR
72	L72.1	JPEG	MILD DR
	L72.2	JPEG	MILD DR
	R72.3	JPEG	MILD DR
	R72.4	JPEG	MILD DR

A. The ―Person‖ attribute is the number of the patient in the dataset.

B. The ―Image number‖ attribute gives the number of images for each patient. **L** indicates Left Eye image and **R** indicates Right eye Image of the patient. All odd number images e.g., LXX.1, RXX.3 are OCTA images and Even number Images e.g., LXX.2, RXX.4 are Fundus Images of Patients

C. The ―Image Format‖ attribute shows the format of the image (.jpg).

D. The ―Classification Status‖ attribute shows the classification of the DR.

Table 4.3: Categorization of the images within the database

Classification	Number of images	OCTA	Fundus
NO DR	182	91	91
MILD DR	26	13	13
MODERATE DR	14	7	7

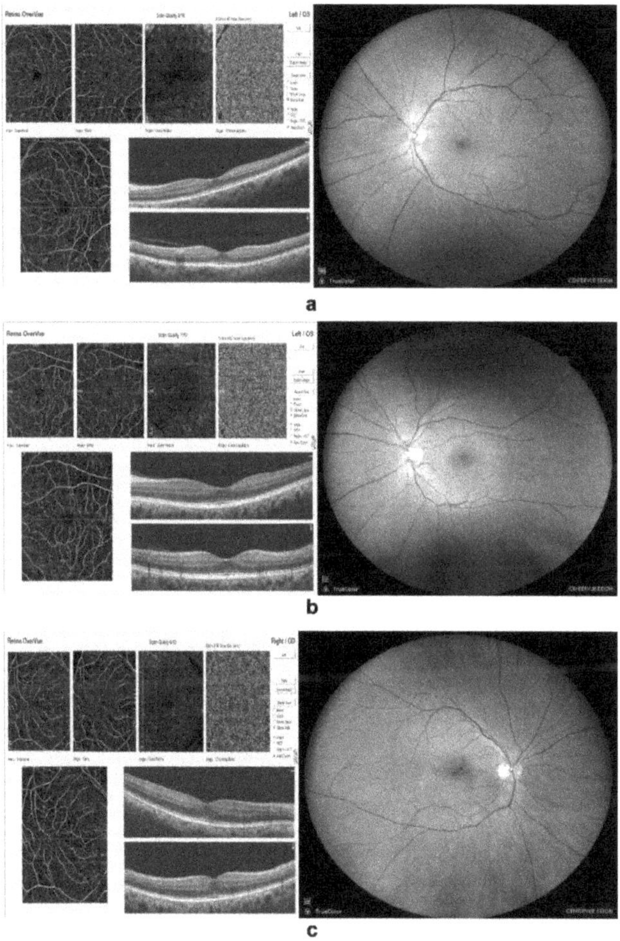

Figure 4.8: Shows OCTA and Fundus images with different stages of DR.

a OCTA and Fundus images with No signs of DR. Fig. 1b OCTA and Fundus images with Mild signs of DR. Fig. 1c OCTA and Fundus images with Moderate signs of DR.

Figure 4.8a provides clear OCTA and Fundus images of the same person with no signs of DR. Microaneurysms, or any other lesions are absent in this case.

Figure 4.8b provides OCTA and Fundus images of the same person with Mild signs of DR. Very few microaneurysms are visible in both the modalities in case of Mild DR.

Figure 4.8c provides OCTA and Fundus images of the same person with Moderate signs of DR. In this type of DR, microaneurysms, along with retinal haemorrhages or exudates are visible.

4. Experimental Design, Materials and Methods

In this study total of 222 OCTA and Fundus images were obtained from individuals over the age of 30 years and above through a specific process. Cataract patients of similar age groups wherein some of them have diabetes and some of them don't have diabetes also some patients who have had diabetes for a very long time are considered. Post Operatively on Day-15 when individuals come for the second follow-up their OCTA and Fundus Scans are taken at Natasha Eye Care and Research Institute Pune. The described procedure is outlined as follows:

1. Patients undergo an interview, during which their information is documented in a patient file, including a checklist to document details regarding the patient's age and diabetes history. Additional health conditions or concurrent illnesses such as hypertension, ischemic heart disease (IHD), or the type of medication they are using, which may include oral pills, insulin, or a combination of both.
2. For advanced cases, systemic factors play a crucial role, including conditions like nephropathy, neuropathy, retinopathy, cardiomyopathy, vasculopathy, gastroparesis, and skin issues.
3. OCTA Images were obtained as 8 × 8 mm2 in size, centered on the macula, and images of superficial capillary plexus (SCP), Deep capillary plexus (DCP), and full thickness retinal slab are taken from Optovue Avanti Edition OCTA Machine with the Specifications: Machine Name: RTVue XR 100

Avanti Edition, FOV 32° (H) x 22° (V), Monochrome CCD Camera: WVGA 1/3° CCD Format, NIR Illumination: 735 nm LED.

4. Fundus Scans are taken using Eidon machine with the Specifications as Centervue Eidon UWF Confocal SLO, Pupil size- 2.5mm, 110 ° wide view scanning technique in automatic mode & 150° in manual mode.
5. The determination of diabetic retinopathy stage is determined by a retina specialist. During the assessment of acquired retinographies, pictures that are out of focus, contain artifacts, or exhibit low image quality due to issues like low signal strength are excluded.
6. Additionally, retinographies from patients with any other retina treatment, patients with macular edema [6], and macular drusens, Proliferative Diabetic Retinopathy Patients, post-laser patients, and PVD (Posterior Vitreous Detachments) patients are not incorporated.

Limitations

Describing the research and obtaining patients' consent poses a significant challenge [[7], [8]]. Additionally, performing an OCTA scan requires expert guidance because it necessitates more patient cooperation to achieve optimal clarity. This study is limited to 222 multimodal images, which includes 111 OCTA images and 111 Fundus images of 76 patients.

Ethics Statement

The study was approved by the Symbiosis Institutional Ethics Committee (BHR) SIU with approval number SIU/IEC/583. Every patient provided informed consent for both treatment and examination taken by the Department of Ophthalmology at Natasha Eye Care and Research Institute. Data is protected by a data usage agreement. The patients' identities remain undisclosed, and the confidentiality of their medical conditions is rigorously maintained.

CRediT authorship contribution statement

Pooja Bidwai: Conceptualization, Investigation, Data curation, Writing – original draft, Visualization.

Shilpa Gite: Conceptualization, Investigation, Visualization, Writing – review & editing.

Aditi Gupta: Investigation, Resources, Data curation, Writing – review & editing, Visualization.
Kishore Pahuja: Conceptualization, Validation, Resources, Project administration.
Ketan Kotecha: Validation, Writing – review & editing.

Acknowledgements

This research is funded by Symbiosis International University.

Declaration of Competing Interest

The authors declare that they have no known competing financial interests or personal relationships that could have appeared to influence the work reported in this paper.

Contributor Information

Shilpa Gite, Email: shilpa.gite@sitpune.edu.in.
Ketan Kotecha, Email: director@sitpune.edu.in.

Data Availability

Multimodal OCTA and Fundus Image dataset for detection of Diabetic Retinopathy (Version-1) (Original data) (Multimodal OCTA and Fundus Image dataset for detection of Diabetic Retinopathy (Version-1))

4.3.3 Analysis of Performance

A detailed comparative assessment was performed to assess the effectiveness of the proposed ImGLN-TL+Bi-LSTM-SN approach for the early detection and advanced prediction of DR. The assessment was carried out in two states such as Detection of DR and Progressive DR Prediction. Various performance measures such as Specificity, F-measure, Accuracy, FDR, Precision, MCC, Sensitivity, FNR, NPV and FPR were measured in this valuation. To further evaluate the proposed ImGLN-TL+Bi-LSTM-SN method, other analyses like a study on Ablation, Statistical Analysis, AUC-ROC curve analysis and Confusion Matrix were performed. The ImGLN-TL structure was compared to other traditional methods such as Bi-GRU, VGG-19 [106], DCNN, DkSO-Light GBM [105], GoogleNet,

SqueezeNet and LeNet. Also, the Bi-LSTM-SN method was compared with standard methods such as LinkNet, Bi-LSTM, SqueezeNet CNN and EfficientNet.

4.3.4 Analysis of Pre-processing

The original Fundus and OCT images with their preprocessing via Anisotropic, Gaussian, Median and Wiener filters is depicting in **Figure 4.9** and **Figure 4.10**. Among these, the Gaussian filter produced the most effective pre-processing outcomes, which is superior to the others with respect to image clarity and quality.

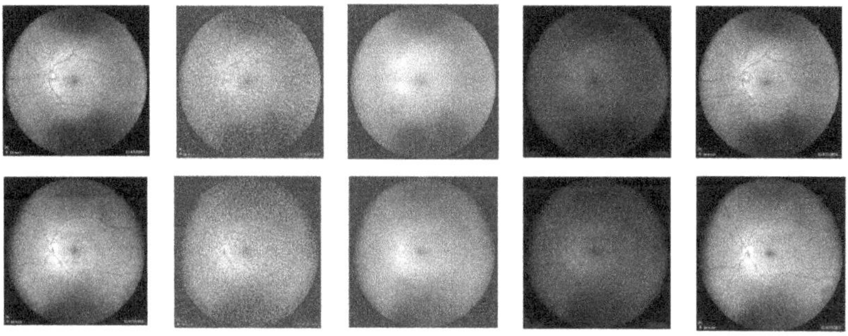

(a) (b) (c) (d) (e)

Figure 4.9: Pre-processed Fundus Images a) Original Images b) Anisotropic c) Median d) Wiener and e) Gaussian

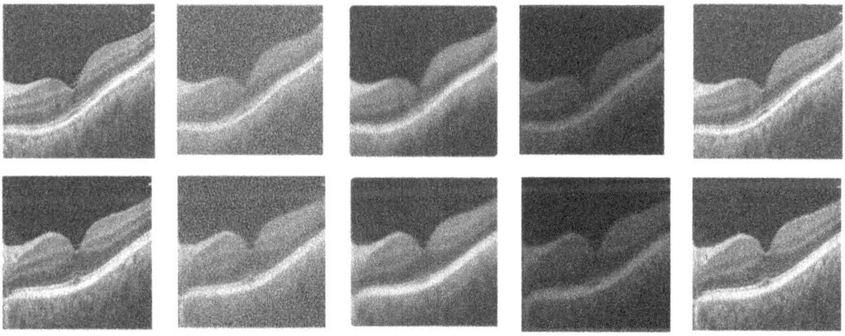

(a) (b) (c) (d) (e)

Figure 4.10: Pre-processed OCT Images a) Original Images b) Anisotropic c) Median d) Wiener and e) Gaussian

4.3.5 Segmentation Analysis

Figure 4.11 and **Figure 4.12** proves the original Fundus and OCT images with their segmented process by four different methods such as ImResUNet, FCM, Conventional ResUNet and K-Means. It highlights each method performs in segmentation tasks. Among them, ImResUNet refers by providing superior outcomes, especially with respect to segmentation precision, better edge explanation and its ability to achieve complex structures more effectively in Fundus as well as OCT images.

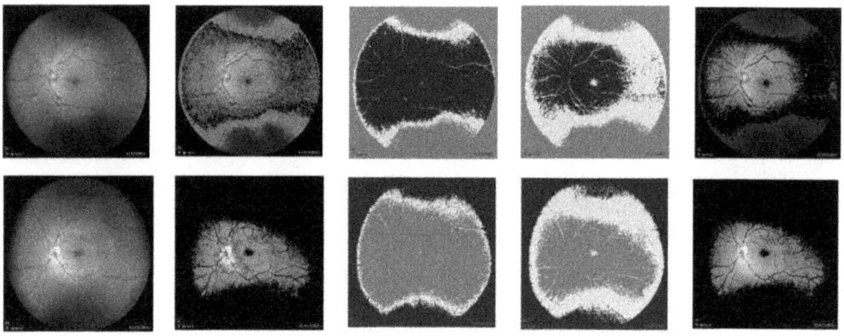

(i) (ii) (iii) (iv) (v)

Figure 4.11: Segmented Fundus Images a) Pre-processed Images b) Conventional ResUNet c) FCM d) K-Means e) ImResUNet

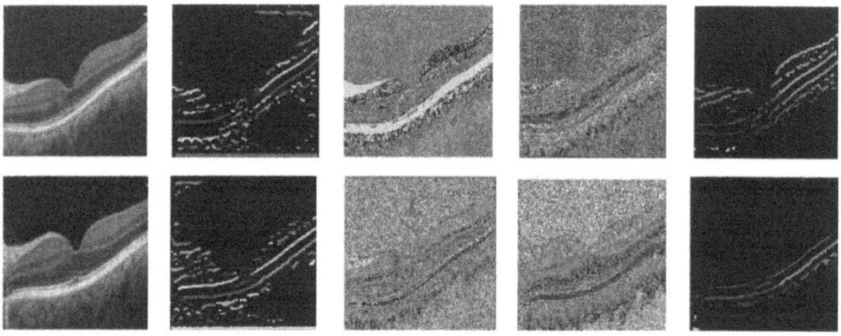

(i) (ii) (iii) (iv) (v)

Figure 4.12: Segmented outcomes for OCT Images a) Pre-processed Images b) Conventional ResUNet c) FCM d) K-Means e) ImResUNet

4.3.5.1 Evaluation of Segmentation Models

Segmentation analysis of ImResUNet is present in **Table 4.4** and **Table 4.5**, which compares its performance with Conventional FCM, K-means, and ResUNet for OCT Fundus and images. According to **Table 4.4**, the output demonstrated that ImResUNet obtained the highest Dice score (0.913), its superior ability to segment Fundus images effectively. The segmented outcome score for the conventional approaches such as FCM is 0.587, K-Means is 554 and Conventional ResUNet is 0.857, which yielded lower Dice scores.

The ImResUNet reached a peak score (0.871 as assessing the Jaccard index for OCT images, whereas Jaccard scores obtained for K-Means is 0.569, Conventional ResUNet is 0.771 and FCM is 0.567. These outcomes highlight the improved segmentation performance of ImResUNet. The integration of residual blocks and a novel self-attention mechanism contributes to a more precise and context-aware segmentation of retinal structures in both Fundus and OCT images.

Table 4.4: Assessment of Various Segmentation Models on Fundus Images

Measures	Jaccard	Dice
FCM	0.508	0.587
K-Means	0.434	0.554
Conventional ResUNet	0.716	0.857
ImResUNet	0.86	0.913

Table 4.5: Assessment of Various Segmentation Models on OCT Images

Measures	Jaccard	Dice
FCM	0.567	0.627
K-Means	0.569	0.618
Conventional ResUNet	0.771	0.85
ImResUNet	0.871	0.913

4.3.6 Analysis of Detection Performance

4.3.6.1 Analysis of Comparisons

A comparative analysis was conducted for early diabetic retinopathy detection to assess the ImGLN-TL model effectiveness. This assessment compared the performance of the ImGLN-TL model with several standard methods such as Bi-GRU, VGG-19 [106], DCNN, DkSO-Light GBM [105], GoogleNet, SqueezeNet and LeNet. **Figure 4.13**, **Figure 4.14** and **Figure 4.15** demonstrates the outcomes of this analysis. It must demonstrate higher scores in both positive and neutral measures for a model to effectively detect diabetic retinopathy, which represents its reliability and accuracy. According to Precision metric, the ImGLN-TL model consistently outperformed the traditional methods.

Particularly, the training data at 80%, ImGLN-TL obtained an impressive precision rate (0.976), which exceeds the precision values of Bi-GRU of 0.899, VGG-19 [106]of 0.897, DCNN of 0.927, DkSO-Light GBM [105] of 0.915, GoogleNet of 0.894, SqueezeNet of 0.864 and LeNet of 0.876. Furthermore, at 90% training data, the ImGLN-TL model attained the highest specificity (0.978), representing its robust performance in accurately identifying diabetic retinopathy. In contrast, the conventional approaches displayed lower specificity values, ranging between 0.865 and 0.936.

The ImGLN-TL achieved the highest F-measure (0.925) with 60% training data, which outperforms the traditional methods. The F-measure scores of the ImGLN-TL improved to 0.932 at 70% training data and 0.942 at 80% training data. The F-measure reached 0.967 at 90% training data, while the traditional methods, including Bi-GRU, VGG-19 [106], DCNN, DkSO-Light GBM [105], GoogleNet, SqueezeNet and LeNet, showed lower F-measure values. A critical factor for effective diabetic retinopathy detection is minimizing the negative metric values.

According to the FDR metric, the ImGLN-TL achieved the lowest error rate (0.026) with 90% training data. In comparison, higher error rates with FDR values of VGG-19 [106]is 0.083 and DCNN is 0.075, while DkSO-Light GBM [105] is 0.065 and SqueezeNet is 0.063. LeNet and Bi-GRU showed FDR values of 0.051 and 0.052, respectively. The ImGLN-TL model includes a dual-network configuration and a log-cosh focal Dice loss function, which enhances convergence, addresses class imbalance and progresses classification robustness.

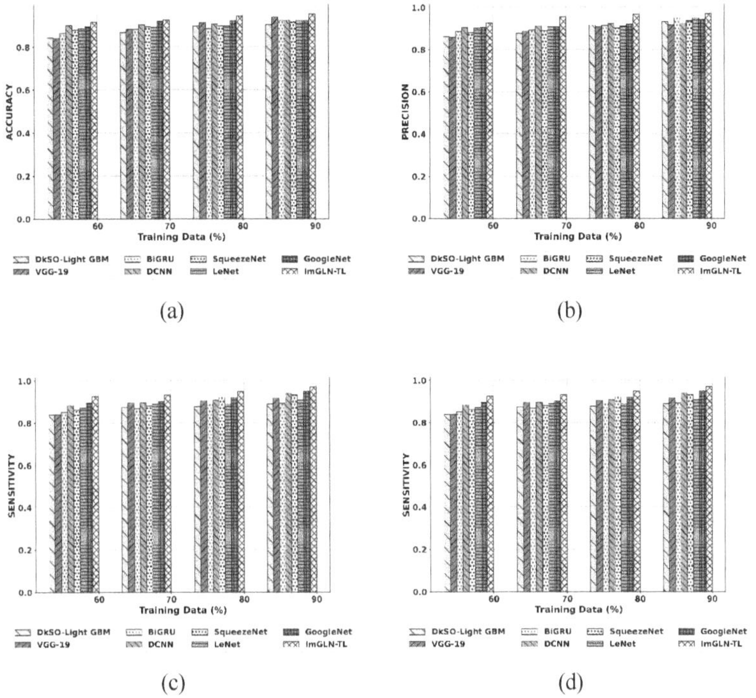

Figure 4.13: Positive Metric Comparison for ImGLN-TL Versus Traditional Methods: a) Accuracy, b) Precision, c) Sensitivity, d) Specificity

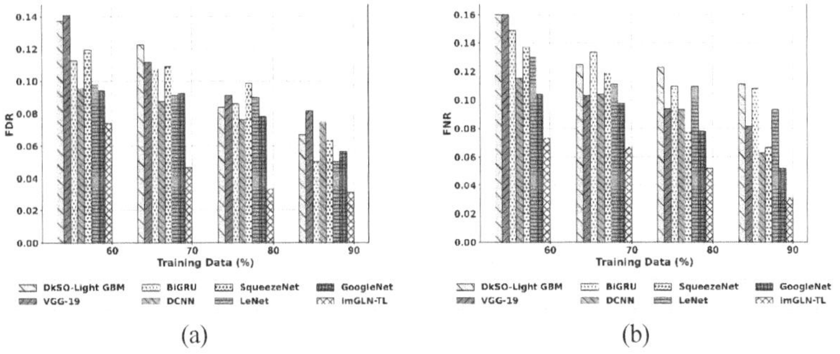

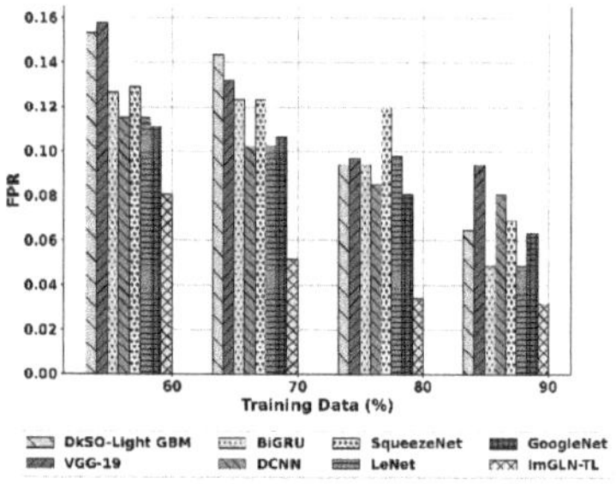

(c)

Figure 4.14: Negative Metrics Comparison for ImGLN-TL Versus Traditional Methods: a) FDR b) FNR and c) FPR

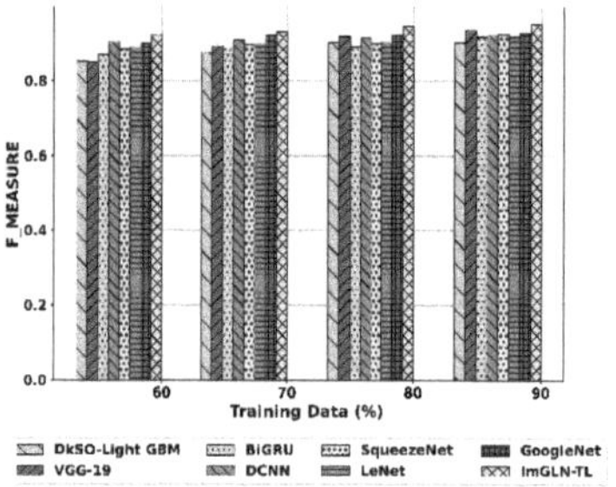

(a)

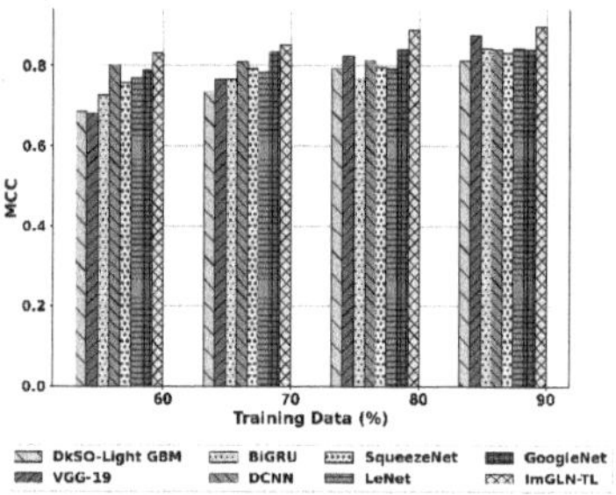

(b)

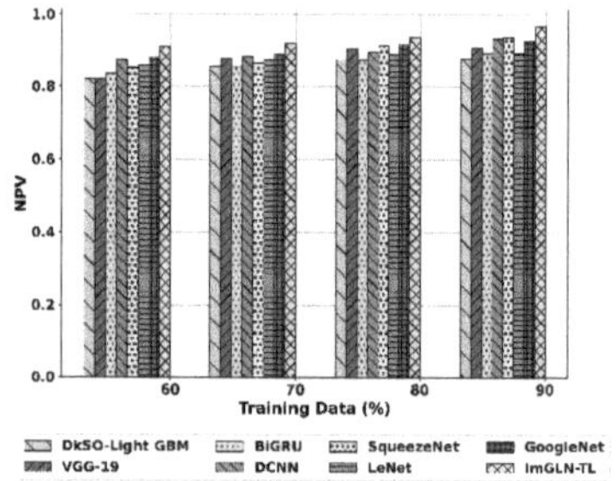

(c)

Figure 4.15: Neutral Metrics Comparison for ImGLN-TL Versus Traditional Methods: a) F-measure b) MCC and c) NPV

4.3.6.2 AUC-ROC Curve Evaluation

AUC-ROC is utilized to assess the performance of binary classification models. The AUC score ranges from 0 to 1, where 1 specifies perfect classification and 0.5 suggests performance no better than random guessing. In this study, the AUC-ROC performance of the ImGLN-TL model for early diabetic retinopathy detection is compared with several existing methods, including Bi-GRU, VGG-19 [106], DCNN, DkSO-Light GBM [105], GoogleNet, SqueezeNet and LeNet, as shown in **Figure 4.16**.

The ImGLN-TL model attained the highest AUC of 0.94, which shows superior performance in early diabetic retinopathy detection. In comparison, GoogleNet and LeNet attained AUC values of 0.92 and 0.90 respectively, which are strong but still lower than the ImGLN-TL model's performance. Other methods, such as Bi-GRU, DkSO-Light GBM [105], SqueezeNet, VGG-19 [106] and DCNN produced AUC values ranging from 0.87 to 0.89, indicating solid performance but not surpassing the ImGLN-TL model. These outcomes highlight the superior ability of the ImGLN-TL model's to accurately detect diabetic retinopathy at an early stage. Additionally, the ImSLBT is designed to capture fine-grained texture variations and is robust to changes in lighting situations.

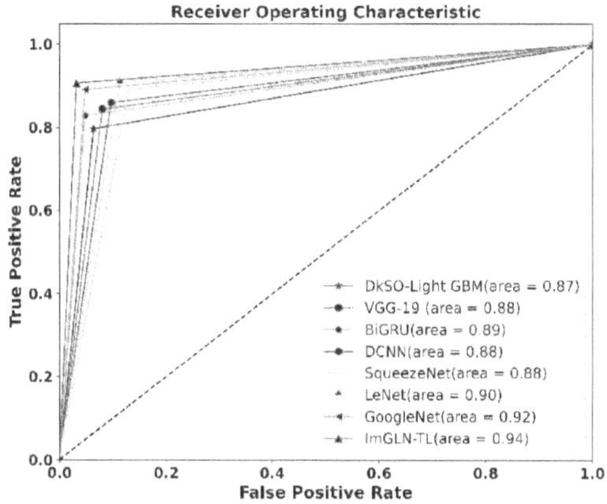

Figure 4.16: Comparative AUC-ROC Analysis for ImGLN-TL and Traditional Approaches

4.3.6.3 Analysis of Accuracy from a Statistical Perspective

A comprehensive statistical assessment of the ImGLN-TL model is conducted to assess its performance compared to existing methods such as Bi-GRU, VGG-19 [106], DCNN, DkSO-Light GBM [105], GoogleNet, SqueezeNet and LeNet. This comparison aims to measure the effectiveness of the ImGLN-TL model for early diabetic retinopathy detection. The outcomes of this comparison are presented in **Table 4.6**, which offered a thorough overview of the efficiency of model relative to these traditional methods.

With respect to Median Statistical Metric, the ImGLN-TL model achieved the highest accuracy of 0.935, indicating a substantial improvement in retinopathy detection performance. In comparison, traditional methods such as Bi-GRU, VGG-19 [106], DCNN, DkSO-Light GBM [105], GoogleNet, SqueezeNet and LeNet showed lower accuracy values, which ranges 0.882 to 0.919.

Furthermore, under the Maximum Statistical Metric, the ImGLN-TL model again outperformed the others, which obtained an accuracy rate of 0.951. As a result, the accuracy of the other methods, including Bi-GRU, VGG-19 [106], DCNN, DkSO-Light GBM [105], GoogleNet, SqueezeNet and LeNet, ranged from 0.905 to 0.937. These results highlight the ImGLN-TL model's superior performance in the early detection of diabetic retinopathy.

Table 4.6: Analysis of Accuracy from a Statistical Perspective

Statistical Measures	Standard Deviation	Minimum	Median	Maximum	Mean
Bi-GRU	0.021	0.863	0.884	0.921	0.888
VGG-19 [106]	0.036	0.841	0.898	0.937	0.894
DCNN	0.007	0.901	0.906	0.921	0.908
DkSO-Light GBM [105]	0.024	0.843	0.882	0.905	0.878
GoogleNet	0.011	0.895	0.919	0.921	0.914
SqueezeNet	0.013	0.879	0.896	0.917	0.897
LeNet	0.013	0.885	0.895	0.921	0.899
ImGLN-TL	0.014	0.917	0.935	0.951	0.935

4.3.7 Analysis of Sequential Prediction Accuracy

4.3.7.1 Analysis of Comparisons

A detailed comparison of the Bi-LSTM-SN strategy against traditional methods is illustrating in **Table 4.7** for the progressive prediction of diabetic retinopathy. The outcomes show that the Bi-LSTM-SN model consistently outperforms the established methods across various evaluation metrics, demonstrating its superior ability to accurately predict diabetic retinopathy. Specifically, the Bi-LSTM-SN achieved an NPV (0.931), which highlights its strong capability in predicting the condition. In comparison, traditional approaches achieved lower NPV values od CNN is 0.840, EfficientNet is 0.824, LinkNet is 0.812, Bi-LSTM is 0.893and SqueezeNet is 0.892.

Also, the Bi-LSTM-SN model achieved a sensitivity rate (0.946), which reflects its excellent performance in correctly recognizing diabetic retinopathy. As a reults, the sensitivity rates for LinkNet, EfficientNet, CNN, SqueezeNet and Bi-LSTM were lower. The Bi-LSTM component captures temporal dependencies, while SqueezeNet focuses on reducing spatial features and their combined outcome provides the final prediction of diabetic retinopathy over time.

Table 4.7: Evaluation of Bi-LSTM-SN Against Traditional Models

Metrics	BiLSTM	LinkNet	EfficientNet	SqueezeNet	CNN	Bi-LSTM-SN
F-Measure	0.91	0.87	0.829	0.901	0.878	**0.94**
Sensitivity	0.919	0.812	0.838	0.894	0.879	**0.946**
FDR	0.103	0.128	0.179	0.074	0.11	**0.057**
NPV	0.893	0.812	0.824	0.892	0.84	**0.931**
Accuracy	0.908	0.862	0.823	0.9	0.882	**0.938**
FNR	0.081	0.188	0.162	0.106	0.121	**0.054**
MCC	0.812	0.732	0.646	0.8	0.772	**0.877**
Precision	0.897	0.872	0.821	0.926	0.89	**0.943**
Specificity	0.891	0.872	0.813	0.922	0.883	**0.947**
FPR	0.109	0.128	0.188	0.078	0.117	**0.053**

4.3.7.2 Confusion Matrix Metrics Evaluation

A confusion matrix is a tool used to assess the performance of a classification system by displaying the counts of TP, TN, FP and FN. These values help evaluate how well a model predicts different classes, with TP and TN representing correct predictions, and FP and FN indicating incorrect ones. The performance of the Bi-LSTM-SN model for diabetic retinopathy prediction is thoroughly analyzed using a confusion matrix, as depicting in **Figure 4.17**. This matrix compares the Bi-LSTM-SN model's performance with traditional methods such as CNN, EfficientNet, LinkNet, Bi-LSTM, and SqueezeNet.

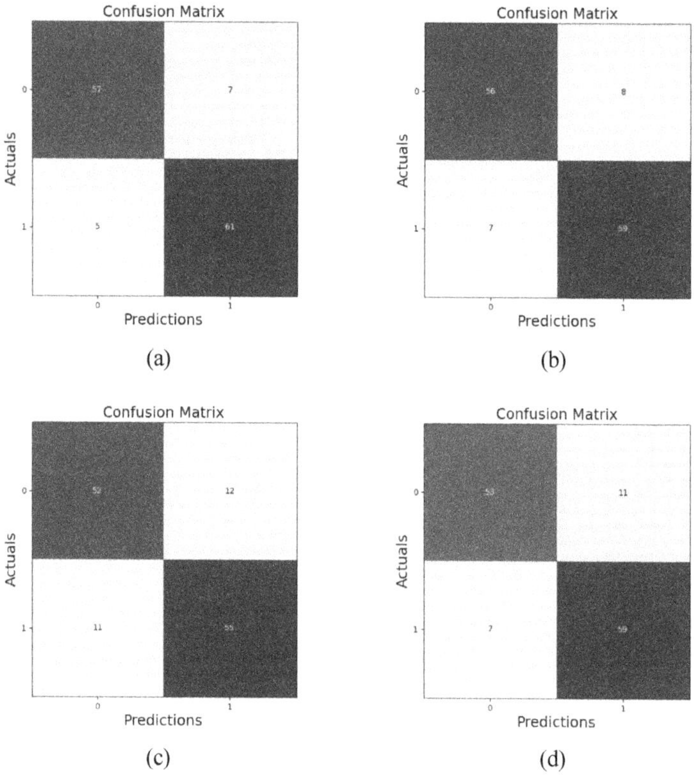

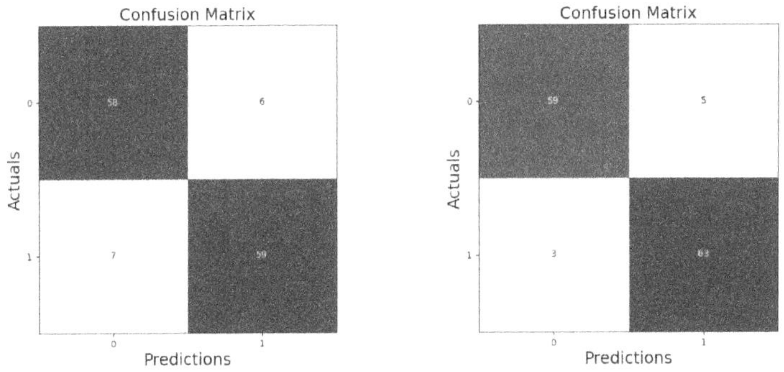

(e) (f)

Figure 4.17: Confusion Matrix Assessment for Bi-LSTM-SN and Traditional Models a) Bi-LSTM b) CNN c) EfficientNet d) LinkNet e) SqueezeNet and f) Bi-LSTM-SN

According to TN, the Bi-LSTM-SN model achieved the highest performance with a TN rate of 59, indicating its excellent ability to accurately identify diabetic retinopathy. In comparison, the traditional methods had TN values of Bi-LSTM (56), CNN (52), EfficientNet (53), LinkNet (58) and SqueezeNet (59). Moreover, the Bi-LSTM-SN model recorded the lowest FN score of 3, while EfficientNet had a higher FN score (11). The Bi-LSTM, CNN, LinkNet, and SqueezeNet models each had FN scores of 7.

4.3.8 Ablation Analysis

According to an ablation analysis, different components of a model are systematically removed to observe how these changes affect its overall performance. The results of an ablation study for the ImGLN-TL+Bi-LSTM-SN strategy was illustrating in **Table 4.8**, which evaluates its effectiveness in the early detection and prediction of diabetic retinopathy in comparison to several alternative variations. The comparison includes variations such as ImGLN-TL+Bi-LSTM-SN with Fundus images only, ImGLN-TL+Bi-LSTM-SN with OCT images only, ImGLN-TL+Bi-LSTM-SN excluding feature extraction, ImGLN-TL+Bi-LSTM-SN using standing segmentation, ImGLN-TL+Bi-LSTM-SN with existing feature extraction, and ImGLN-TL+Bi-LSTM-SN using existing GoogleNet.

The ImGLN-TL+Bi-LSTM-SN method achieved the highest accuracy (0.944), which significantly outperforming the other variations. Specifically, ImGLN-TL+Bi-LSTM-SN excluding feature extraction and ImGLN-TL+Bi-LSTM-SN with Fundus images only achieved accuracy rates of 0.829 and 0.835, respectively. The ImGLN-TL+Bi-LSTM-SN with OCT images only and the ImGLN-TL+Bi-LSTM-SN using existing segmentation both achieved accuracy rates of 0.841, while ImGLN-TL+Bi-LSTM-SN with existing feature extraction score of 0.853. The ImGLN-TL+Bi-LSTM-SN using existing GoogleNet showed a slight improvement, reaching an accuracy (0.921), nonetheless still did not surpass the performance of the full ImGLN-TL+Bi-LSTM-SN approach.

Table 4.8: Assessment of the ImGLN-TL+Bi-LSTM-SN Approach with Different Image and Processing Variants

Metrics	ImGLN-TL+Bi-LSTM-SN with Fundus images only	ImGLN-TL+Bi-LSTM-SN with Existing Segmentation	ImGLN-TL+Bi-LSTM-SN with Existing GoogleNet	ImGLN-TL+Bi-LSTM-SN with Existing Feature Extraction	ImGLN-TL+Bi-LSTM-SN with OCT images only	ImGLN-TL+Bi-LSTM-SN without Feature Extraction	ImGLN-TL+Bi-LSTM-SN
NPV	0.819	0.815	0.919	0.808	0.824	0.814	0.937
FPR	0.171	0.148	0.081	0.103	0.162	0.179	0.034
F-Measure	0.845	0.849	0.922	0.856	0.851	0.84	0.947
Sensitivity	0.841	0.832	0.922	0.815	0.844	0.837	0.948
FDR	0.15	0.133	0.078	0.098	0.143	0.157	0.033
Specificity	0.829	0.852	0.919	0.897	0.838	0.821	0.966
FNR	0.159	0.168	0.078	0.185	0.156	0.163	0.052
Precision	0.85	0.867	0.922	0.902	0.857	0.843	0.967
MCC	0.669	0.683	0.841	0.711	0.681	0.657	0.89
Accuracy	0.835	0.841	0.921	0.853	0.841	0.829	0.944

Moreover, the ImGLN-TL+Bi-LSTM-SN model achieved a false positive rate (FPR) of 0.034, which was notably lower than the other variations. For comparison, ImGLN-TL+Bi-LSTM-SN with Fundus images only had an FPR of 0.171, ImGLN-TL+Bi-LSTM-SN with OCT images only had 0.162, and ImGLN-TL+Bi-LSTM-SN excluding feature extraction had an FPR of 0.179. The ImGLN-TL+Bi-LSTM-SN using existing segmentation, ImGLN-TL+Bi-LSTM-SN with existing feature extraction, and ImGLN-TL+Bi-LSTM-SN with existing GoogleNet exhibited FPRs of 0.148, 0.103, and 0.081, respectively, which were higher than the full ImGLN-TL+Bi-LSTM-SN approach.

4.4 Summary

In this research, a comprehensive framework for DR detection and progression prediction was developed. Firstly, OCT and fundus images underwent preprocessing using Gaussian filtering to enhance image quality. Next, the ImResU-Net model, prepared with an improved attention mechanism, was employed for precise segmentation, preserving critical contextual information. Succeeding segmentation, significant features were extracted, including deep and statistical features for OCT images and PHOG and ImSLBT for fundus images. These features were then combined through a novel left-to-right fusion approach to form a comprehensive feature set.

An ImGLN-TL was applied for detection, which incorporated an enhanced inception module and a log-cosh focal Dice loss function to address gradient issues and overfitting challenges. To predict disease progression, a hybrid SqueezeNet and Bi-LSTM model was used to capture temporal dependencies and spatial patterns, respectively. The combination of these methods led to improved accuracy, robustness, and reliability in diagnosing and predicting diabetic retinopathy. The ImGLN-TL model achieved the highest specificity rate of 0.978 with 90% training data, demonstrating its superior performance in detecting diabetic retinopathy. In contrast, traditional methods such as Bi-GRU, VGG-19 [106], DCNN, DkSO-Light GBM [105] GoogleNet, SqueezeNet and LeNet showed lower specificity values, ranging from 0.865 to 0.936.

Chapter 5
Conclusion and Future Scope

5.2 Future Scope

The future of diabetic retinopathy (DR) detection and prediction lies in the continued integration of advanced technologies and improved models. As the field evolves, the following areas hold significant potential for further research and development:

- Should explore the combination of various imaging modalities to enhance the accuracy of DR detection. Developing models that integrate these diverse image types could lead to a more comprehensive understanding of the disease for improving early diagnosis and prognosis.
- While deep learning models such as CNNs have shown high accuracy in DR detection, their "black-box" nature remains a challenge in clinical settings. Future work could focus on developing explainable AI models that not only provide predictions but also offer clear, understandable reasoning for those predictions, increasing trust and adoption in clinical practice.
- With the rapid advancements in edge computing and mobile technologies, real-time DR detection systems could be deployed in remote or underserved areas. These systems would use portable devices such as smartphones or handheld fundus cameras combined with AI-based models to provide immediate diagnosis and reducing the need for specialized equipment.
- Incorporating AI-based DR detection systems with existing EHR platforms could streamline the diagnosis process and ensure continuous monitoring of diabetic patients. This integration would allow healthcare providers to track DR progression over time and initiate timely interventions based on automated predictions.

By focusing on these areas, future research in DR detection and prediction will continue to enhance diagnostic precision, improve early detection and provide better management strategies, ultimately reducing the impact of DR on global health.

www.ingramcontent.com/pod-product-compliance
Lightning Source LLC
LaVergne TN
LVHW051923051126
851857LV00021B/2110
* 9 7 9 8 2 4 0 8 9 8 7 8 5 *